D0397413

The
Mindset Lists
of
AMERICAN
HISTORY

✳ ✳ ✳ ✳

From Typewriters to
Text Messages, What Ten Generations
of Americans Think Is Normal

Tom McBride and Ron Nief

WILEY
John Wiley & Sons, Inc.

Published by John Wiley & Sons, Inc., Hoboken, New Jersey
Published simultaneously in Canada

For general information about our other products and services, please contact our Customer Care Department within the United States at (800) 762–2974, outside the United States at (317) 572–3993 or fax (317) 572–4002.

Wiley also publishes its books in a variety of electronic formats. Some content that appears in print may not be available in electronic books. For more information about Wiley products, visit our web site at www.wiley.com.

ISBN 978-0-470-87623-7 (cloth); ISBN 978-1-118-01795-1 (ebk); ISBN 978-1-118-01796-8 (ebk); ISBN 978-1-118-01797-5

Printed in the United States of America
10   9   8   7   6   5   4   3   2   1

To Alex and Emma and Alex and Abigail
and to our students and colleagues at Beloit College,
all of whom inspired us with their Mindset Moments

The past is a foreign country; they do things
differently there.

—*L. P. Hartley*

The past is never dead. It's not even past.

—*William Faulkner*

CONTENTS

ACKNOWLEDGMENTS

The Mindset List project extends back to an experimental list created at Beloit College in 1997. A group of colleagues, including Beloit's Institutional Research director Richard Miller, contributed to that list, which launched the phenomenon that has now become the much anticipated annual assessment of the event horizons of eighteen-year-olds. Family, friends, and colleagues have contributed to this process, and we would like to thank Sarah McBride and Joanna Kutter for patience and understanding and no small number of suggestions in the course of assembling the manuscript. Our children, Abigail Van Hoewyk and Alex Nief and Emma and Alex McBride, to whom this book is dedicated, have contributed in innumerable ways.

We extend a special thanks to Beloit College president Scott Bierman and our colleagues at Beloit who have offered encouragement and support. In particular, we wish to thank the following people: David Heesen and Jenny Tschudy for their assistance in the preparation of the manuscript, and Andrew Alt (Beloit '86), Kyle Dallman (Beloit '13), and Beloit Professor Emeritus Art Robson for reading portions of the manuscript. Special thanks to Gayle Keefer and the late William Keefer for their support of the Keefer Chair in the Humanities.

And we have been extremely fortunate to work with literary agent Steven Harris of CSG Literary Partners and with one of publishing's best editors, Stephen S. Power at Wiley, who together made a challenging process enjoyable.

Generations
Have Always Had
Mindsets

In 1998 we launched the first Mindset List from Beloit College as a way to give our faculty and staff some insight into the worldview of the incoming class of students, the men and women who would graduate in 2002. With our list of what has "always" or "never" been true for that class, we detailed the events and new technologies that marked the formative years of these incoming students. We offered a sense of what it was like for them to grow up: the trends and values that to them had always seemed normal. Just one year later, we were amazed at how we seemed to have struck a nerve: the website on which the list was located had become one of the most frequently visited at the college. Now the list, on its own dedicated website, gets more than a million hits each year. Since that first list, we have talked with hundreds of people—journalists and non-journalists, educators and non-educators, parents and students—about the

1

lists and their responses to them. There are lots of reasons why people love the list and look forward to it every year. Among the more important is that older readers perceive an ongoing drama in which they have played a role. The members of each generation are inevitably influenced by what they have seen and heard during their earlier years. Just as high school graduates in 1898 could not imagine a southern president in the White House ever again, and just as high school graduates in 1957 could not imagine life without zippers or the possibility that a "mouse" would ever be anything other than a rodent or a cartoon character, so those in 2009 cannot imagine having to enter phone booths and deposit coins in order to call someone from a street corner. And if the grandchildren of those born today accuse their grandparents of not having done enough to protect the rights of animals, Grandpa and Grandma may be astounded in 2065 at how weird their grandkids and other young people have become.

The Mindset List came into being in response to dispiriting lists circulating on the nascent Internet that indicated how little high school graduates were aware of. Perhaps these glum lists represented a Baby Boomer defense against the encroaching digital generation. In contrast, the Mindset List took the approach that these students were new to serious learning and had to be recognized by their life experiences—those things that had always or had never been part of their lives. It became a topic of conversation, particularly among colleagues responsible for our first year programs, which then slowly spread into available cyberspace. Soon we were surprised to hear from other colleges and then from the media . . . and the rest is history. Based on research through which we immerse ourselves in American culture, especially relating to the early years of class members' lives, and supplemented by suggestions from students and "grown-ups" from all over the world, the annual List has become known as a go-to source for the attitudes and expectations of and a prompt for stories regarding American college students. In this book we have used these methods to illuminate not only generations going back to the late nineteenth century but also future ones of the twenty-first. Each generation has its particular set of expectations, and every generation seems, if not disappointed, at least perplexed when things don't turn out the way they thought they would.

Each has sensed itself as "new" or "now," only to live long enough to be considered quaint. We get old too soon and smart too late. Each year the Mindset List brings this reality home. It is a perpetual drama, deeply rooted in the spectacle of human hopes, human achievement, and human folly. Every generation has its moments of greatness, and of silliness and error. This drama seems perpetual and universal. People worldwide can't seem to get enough of it, and some of them wait eagerly for the renewal of this drama annually with the Mindset List. This book will give them much more of it.

While the Mindset Lists limit their focus to the first eighteen years of each generation, "eighteen" has not always meant what it means today. In 2011 an eighteen-year-old may well be someone who is not expected to become a fully productive member of American society until she or he is twenty-two, if then. For almost half of the current generation, going to college is a norm. Over one-quarter of them finish college. But just one hundred years ago only a tiny fraction of America's young people, mostly white males of a certain status, went to college. Just seventy years ago it was not unusual for schooling to stop at eighth grade. As recently as the 1930s about the same percentage that graduates from college today only finished high school. Before they were eighteen, most young people had already gone to work full-time: in the fields, in the factories, or in the homes of others. Except for a brief period during the 1920s, there was little sense of a special culture of youth until about 1960, by which time young people had, in large numbers, plenty of disposable income. Other generations had little sense of themselves as a special, identifiable generation, with their own brand of music and tastes. The first eighteen years has always been a formative period in which people are likely to be influenced by immediate events and trends. But just as once upon a time people actually dialed telephones (rather than just pushing buttons and calling the action dialing), and just as once upon a time there were no telephones, so once upon a time, and not so long ago, "eighteen" did not mean what it means today. Among other things, this book will illuminate the evolution of "eighteen" itself.

The book explores generational life for 150 years: from 1880 to 2030 (for the college class of 2030 we speculate about what their growing-up years will be like). We start with 1880 because many Americans alive today have grandparents or great-grandparents who lived then. Then, starting in 1918, we focus on generations at intervals of thirteen years. By then the American story, prompted by miraculous technology, the struggle for equal rights, and the calamities of war and depression, began to unfold so quickly that each thirteen-year jump represents an eternity of change. This spacing also allows us to zero in on the young people born at the end of the Great War, those born on the eve of World War II, and those who were late teens at the end of World War II. We can drop in on the boomers and spy on the beginnings of both Generation X and

Generation Y. We also outline the generation that has just started college, and we look ahead to 2030.

For each generation we offer a Mindset List and then a narrative dramatizing what it was like to grow up then. We simulate the phenomenon of present-mindedness that guides every generation by offering details in the present tense rather than in the historical past tense. Every chapter is written as though it were composed during the summer following that class's high school commencement.

As readers encounter what it was like to grow up in these different generations, it may be hard for them to imagine themselves living in such an alien time, for life was stunningly different "back then." Conversely, they might conclude that they would have been better suited to a previous time than to their own. For those actually living through these different generations, the time has always seemed contemporary, for when we cannot see the future, we have trouble believing that there will be one and that someday we will all seem old-fashioned.

In the conclusion we offer a retrospective view. While much has remained the same in the panoply of American life, in many ways the past resembles an alien planet where people did things very differently, facing challenges that we can only imagine. Whether in the past, the present, or the future, we are all part of history in the making, and we will do well never to forget that.

Women Have
Always Ridden
Bicycles

Members of this class were born in 1880. If they graduated from high school, they would have done so in 1898. If they attended college (very unlikely), they would have finished in 1902.

Members of this class include Douglas MacArthur, W. C. Fields (born William Claude Dukenfield), and Helen Keller.

English novelist George Eliot; President James Garfield; James Whistler's mother, Anna; and desperado Billy the Kid have always been dead.

Mindset List

1. Youngsters their age have always had about a one in ten chance of graduating from high school.

2. When away on business, their fathers might have sneaked off to enjoy "Ruby Lips" or "Tantalizing Torsos" at the local burlesque establishment.

3. Their parents could go to the Bowery Theater to see *Nellie, the Beautiful Cloak Model*, then stay and have a drink with the actors.

4. Their elders have never thought darkened theaters were morally acceptable.

5. Most kids their age have left school, having gone to work at around the age of fourteen.

6. They've always heard about buffalo chips being used out West for fuel.

7. Sectional rivalries between North and South, East and West, have always been spreading like bumper crops.

8. They've always been eating steak butchered in Chicago from Texas "dogies."

9. Lone cowboys have always been turning into corporate "ranch hands."

10. Dodge City is losing its reputation as a wild and woolly cow town.

11. Many of them have a dead sibling or two.

12. Their roving uncles may have enjoyed shooting dwindling numbers of buffalo from what the Indians call "the Iron Horse."

13. Machines have always talked.

14. Farming and mining have always been "industries."

15. They've always heard how the West is closing up for good.

16. Big cities have always been sordid but fascinating places—with unpaved roads, palatial mansions, crowded firetraps, daring shows, unsightly and smelly sewers, scrumptious restaurants, omnipresent manure, and fantastic orchestras.

17. Typewriters, with their new QWERTY keyboards, have become the new "literary pianos" and are fast making business letters

and other documents copied with perfect
penmanship seem obsolete.

18. Folks have always been intrigued by trained
fleas, mermaids, Siamese twins, and
"egresses."

19. Huck Finn has always had doubts about
"sivilization."

20. Californians have always been trying to put
Chinese laundries out of business.

21. The boys among them have always been told
that women's suffrage may lead to immoral
ticket-splitting and political independence.

22. Cornelius Vanderbilt alone has always hired
more people for his agricultural experiments
than does the entire United States
Department of Agriculture.

23. Women have always ridden bicycles.

24. The very, very rich have always referred to
their seventy-room mansions, with no trace
of irony, as "cottages."

25. They've grown up hearing about the nation's
trauma over the assassination of President
Garfield by that nutty office-seeker.

26. Children and factories have always needed each other.

27. Jim Crow has always created problems for African Americans in the South.

28. In the improbable event that members of this class go to college, they may find that "moral philosophy" is now obsolete.

29. Joseph Pulitzer has always grabbed the attention of their parents with newspaper headlines like BAPTIZED IN BLOOD.

30. Due process has always been used to protect corporations, not freed slaves.

31. Roman Catholics have always been the object of suspicion and fear.

32. The First Lady has always been a college graduate.

33. A gentleman never refers to a lady's "limbs" as "legs."

34. Police have always stopped horse-drawn carriages for speeding.

35. North-South marriages have become only slightly more acceptable.

36. Twilight in Pittsburgh has always come early.

37. Indians have never wanted to quarrel about God.

38. "Bees" have always meant popular gatherings on the Plains.

39. They've grown up perplexed by the claims of "gold bugs" and "silverites," each claiming that their metallic basis for American currency would lead to prosperity and that the other's would lead to ruin.

40. Choosing to dwell in "apartments," such as those in the Dakota in New York City, gentlemen have always been willing "to live on mere shelves beneath a common roof."

41. Urban America has always chosen to stay up later and later.

42. Railroads have always been enjoying their much improved brakes, which have revolutionized their engines' usage and efficiency on all sorts of terrains and helped spread commerce to new regions of the land.

43. They've always been admonished to rise at five in order to thrive.

44. They've been taught that acres of diamonds are just dandy.

45. For much of the nation the whistle to signal quitting time has always been the finest sound in the world.

46. The Knights of Labor have always been riding into oblivion.

47. "Buckwheats" and "hayseeds" have always been ridiculed.

48. Except when it comes to "goos goos," city political machines have always tolerated human frailty.

49. The market for grain and cotton has always been global.

50. Land has always been taxed much more heavily than personal income.

* * * *

The Verdict, *a periodical of the late nineteenth century, once depicted John D. Rockefeller playing with a toy building that looks just like a Federalist government building. Perhaps it's a little piggy bank, for John D. is finding little bags of money—or "boodle"—spilling out of the bottom. He looks ferociously greedy and intense, and the caption has him exclaiming, "What a Funny Little Government!" Millions of Americans furiously believed that Rockefeller and his fellow leviathans of wealth had toyed with the federal and state governments. In the cartoon published in* The Verdict *he is actually fondling the federal government as a toy. Thus he was enjoying a late childhood. In contrast, most children during this period left school at fourteen and went to work. They had hardly any toys, making do with wooden tops that spin, hoops that you hit with a stick to keep them wheeling down the road, and (if they were lucky) kites. The girls played with rag dolls. In this era children were considered to be future adults and not much more. Yet what they experienced in American life was remarkable and unparalleled.*

* * * *

Although fewer than one in ten of them graduated from high school, the class of 1898 has witnessed startling changes in American life—transformations that bred both hatred and confidence. When they were born, the United States was a young country with a serious rift between North and South and a swath of vast resources in soil, timber, and minerals. By the time they graduated from high school, if they did, America was a behemoth of production, making a fair bid to become a world power. There has been only one main constant: standards of respectability have largely remained the same.

Forty years earlier, on the eve of the Civil War, their fathers had aspired to own their own round barn; now their sons aspire to become the boss of many urban men. The West—probably America's Last West—has killed thousands, brought wealth to thousands of others, and enthralled millions. Cities have become polyglot. Impoverished Sicilians never thought of themselves as Italians until they went to New York City, where they discovered they had a lot more in common with Little Italy than with Little Poland. Reconstruction in the South has always been in the past, and the "freedman," though no longer the slave of men, has remained the slave of society. Railroads have found their way to nearly everywhere, so that both the horse and the horse-drawn wagon have become much less important, and the cattle trails have pushed ever farther west. Thin and superstrong steel walls have made skyscrapers possible, and elevators have made the top floors a cinch to get to. Just tell the operator where you want to go.

By the time they were born, there had always been telephones, phonographs, and lightbulbs, however seldom these devices were actually used. Many have chosen not to bear the expense of a telephone "just to talk." If they lived east of the Missouri River, they would have traveled long-distance by rail, but their few counterparts in the West would more likely have done so by stagecoach, with horses changed every ten miles and a home station every fifth stop for grub, liquor, and maybe a room for the night. It would take them five hours to traverse fifty miles this way, and strong tobacco was discouraged in such close quarters and hair oil was to be avoided under such dusty conditions. If a class member grew up in the New West, he or she probably would have attended a small pioneer schoolhouse like the ones put up within days of a settlement, but would have likely had to go far in order to find a high school.

Already, however, thirty-one states require some grammar school attendance, and many Americans believe that graduation from a "high" school will become the great equalizer between rich and poor. Meanwhile, back east they would have grown up celebrating Memorial Days held in late May and seen parading veterans of the Mexican War and maybe even the occasional veteran of the War of 1812. These events have always been tinged with sadness, as moralistic speakers droned on about the nation's losing a sense of sacrifice and gratefulness, but they could also be fun.

They would have had no memory of their bachelor uncle's spending New Year's Day visiting eligible women during "at home" calls, as by the year they were born, the practice was considered disrespectful because of the excessive number of visits. But they will recall the safe drawing-room spookiness of Halloween, which has always been a young person's holiday. Their older brothers and sisters have always been in on the bicycling craze—and now that these students are graduating from high school, so are they. Like many young people in the United States, they have had to endure the opinion of elders that bicycle races on Sundays are sinful, and so is spending money on lamps, bells, and cyclometers. Someone has always been trying to ride a bicycle so fast that he can cover a mile in a minute.

If they should be lucky enough to go to college—out of 400 Americans, 399 have not and most likely never will—they have a good chance of attending a coeducational one, as most of these schools are now. Meanwhile, they've had history, reading, math, spelling, and elocution drilled into their heads, and have had to follow such penmanship rules as "Keep the top of the pen holder pointing to the right shoulder." They have grown up primarily reading traditional newspapers, with earnest reports of events beneath "tombstones," or stacked headlines. The newer papers, such as those published by William Randolph Hearst and, to a lesser extent, Joseph Pulitzer, scream a lot of fabricated news in seventy-two-point type.

They may well have read these newspapers in oversized houses with dormers and cupolas running riot outside (though if they grew up in New York City they might have lived in the new luxury apartments such as the Dakota and the Navarro). These architectural flourishes have always been a salute to the value of tradition and aristocracy. They've also celebrated how new machinery could produce fancy arches and towers on the facades of ordinary homes. Furnished rooms are so crowded with all manner of ornament that moving around has become a small challenge. Stomachs and divans alike are overstuffed. Etiquette has always been as lavishly ruled as penmanship. Virtue and vice are clearly defined and should never be confused with each other.

When the boys grow up, they expect to acquire the virility that can come only from a beard, or at least a thick mustache. Their mothers might have overindulged them with the Little Lord Fauntleroy look of pampered children, but they have sought to outgrow that as soon as their mothers weren't paying attention or the camera had gone away. The girls would graduate from being all that is sugar and spice to becoming stern mistresses of households. Their long hair was a beauty prize, but like everything else it had to be governed, usually in ringlets. Bustles have been de rigueur, but with women now riding bikes, dare anyone think the bustle is doomed?

For entertainment they have always had the circus and Buffalo Bill Cody's Wild West, which has at times drawn around forty thousand people for a single show. They may have attended melodramas on Broadway or in other parts of the country, with their parents. Minstrel and burlesque and even vaudeville variety shows, with their racy jokes and tight-stocking ladies, might well, however, be a bit too daring. Athletics has always been called "sport," and there has always been something a bit unsavory about playing it for money. The boys have always followed professional boxing, though, even if the new requirement of padded gloves has eliminated some of the risk and thus some of the adventure. They may also have tried to throw "basketballs" into "peach baskets," though that's mainly something a YMCA lad might participate in.

If class members live beyond the present era, they will have their own children in the first two decades of the next century. Their grandchildren could be born midcentury, and their great-grandkids could be born around 1980. Yet they themselves have always grown up with infant mortality, and it is hardly unusual for them to have a dead infant sibling, or even two.

* * * *

As they've grown up, they have been surrounded by a variety of intense hatreds—by all sorts of groups against all sorts of other groups. These patterns of mutual loathing persisted regardless of the state of their family life and regardless of American confidence about the vitality of national growth. Their parents also grew up with bitter rivalries as normal, but they were simpler: basically North versus South. The class of 1898 has matured with much more complicated sectional and political resentments. Whether such things ever affected them directly, the daily papers have always covered them all; to them these unhappy trends are part of American life—unless, like young Douglas MacArthur, they have spent most of their time isolated on military bases or in academies. Newspaper accounts, bolstered by new printing presses that can put out thousands of copies in just a few hours, have always carried these sagas of constant spite.

In the cities the Irish machine politicians have always hated the "goos goos," the good-government types who want to scale back favors from city hall and put everything on an "objective" civil footing. But what about the Irish fellow who's lost his job and needs a handout or a break in exchange for a vote? He'll do a good job as an extra sweeping the streets and can always work as a "floater," voting in election wards where he isn't actually registered, in exchange. What's the harm o' that? And what's the peril of having a little drink on Sundays? But the "goos goos," often the old Protestant types, are always in favor of the blue laws. They seem to have little patience for human flaws. And they certainly don't know how to grease the wheels of a big city.

Many of the city bosses have always been Catholic, and when members of the class of 1898 were small children, the American Protective Association launched a campaign of hatred against Catholics, depicting them as the ruination of American cities, a bunch of undesirables who would drink and drive the country to destruction, people who prefer a garish statue of the Virgin to a good Presbyterian sermon. In New England some Protestants have always declined to celebrate Christmas because they have seen it as a "Papist" holiday. Catholics and Chinese alike have always been despised. White laundry owners in California have tried to drive Chinese-owned laundries out of business by applying a double standard in building codes.

Meanwhile, the "labor elites" in the United States—those born here and mainly of white Anglo-Saxon Protestant background—have long hated all manner of immigrants: the Greeks, Czechs, Russians, Romanians, Poles, Italians, and others who came through Castle Garden and then the "isle of tears," Ellis Island, and moved into the crowded and filthy enclaves of New York and other major Eastern cities. The current wave of immigration has always been deemed "new": mothers and fathers of the class of 1898 have always said our immigrants no longer come from Britain, France, and Germany but from southern and eastern Europe, and they are people who talk funny, dress funny, and act funny in all sorts of ways. Their demeanor of fear but also of hope, of cowering while also being patient, is by now quite familiar to Protestants on the East Coast. Very different were the less peculiar "Old" Immigrants, such as the Dukenfield family from Britain, who claimed royal ancestry and birthed class member W. C. Dukenfield, who left home at eleven to become a vaudeville juggler. At fifteen, he adopted "W. C. Fields" as his stage name.

Beyond bosses versus goo-goos and Old America versus New Immigrants, there has always been resentful labor against resentful capital. Andrew Carnegie has never allowed himself to be undersold, and John D. Rockefeller has rarely owned less than 90 percent of the oil refining capacity in the country. Dinner parties for the rich, in what Mark Twain has been calling the Gilded Age, have always meant lavish meals of buffet Russe, columbine of chicken, ruddy duck, and vanilla mousse in the capacious dining halls of seventy-room "cottages." The enterprises of the rich have always been protected by presidents who sent in strikebreakers and by courts that, as in Minnesota, struck down state regulations of a large railroad on the grounds that a corporation was a "person" sheltered by the Fourteenth Amendment. Although labor organizations have always been plumping for Saturdays off (with the same pay) in the name of having something called a "weekend," these machine-age aristocrats have never supported such preposterous ideas.

Mining the coal and butchering the hogs have worked people to death—this has never been a figure of speech—but the big boys have always said that this must be how God wants it.

One of their pastors, Henry Ward Beecher, once said that if a man cannot live on bread and water, he is not fit to live. City families of nine have slept on the floor in two shivering rooms; they have survived on tiny portions of bread, potatoes, and molasses; they have worn tatters for clothes and cardboard for shoes. Yet if not God, then it has always been Mr. Darwin, who must have decreed that only the fit do—and should—survive and prosper. The rich men have always felt that the best way to grow is to put profits back into expansion and not into the men who help make them. In Chicago the mass slaughter of cattle has always been rapid, and reinvestment in new meatpacking plants has always been immediate. Thus the great meatpacking tycoon Mr. Gustavus Franklin Swift has always been swift by name and by nature. He and these other great men have wanted to make not just the "boodle," but also the world.

Labor—in the hodgepodge assortment of moderate union men, anarchists, socialists, and other idealists or malcontents—has never gone along with any of these notions. Some are for free enterprise, but many have always thought that in time capitalism would be the cause of its own downfall by paying its workers so little that there would be no one able to buy the goods. By the time the class of 1898 was in elementary school, the labor movement, thanks in part to a lethal riot in the Haymarket area of Chicago, had become largely discredited. Despite what many have called desperate working conditions, the Knights of Labor, perhaps the country's most important organization for the workingman, has started to seem not perfect and gentle but flawed and violent.

* * * *

Members of the class of 1898 have grown up in a nation divided six ways to Sunday. The Not just classes, but also regions, have been in on the act. The North has always loathed the South, and in the unlikely event that an older brother or sister from Cleveland wanted to marry someone from Savannah, the family would have to "see about that." Republicans in the North have always been "waving the bloody shirt" and reminding voters that it was southern Democrats who spilled the blood of rebellion and betrayal. In the South lynching and poll taxes have inexorably kept blacks away from voting booths. The black-faced clown "Jim Crow," who pretends that everything is really all right amid all that bigotry, has always pervaded the old Confederacy, now mired in strictly enforced regulations governing the lives of black people.

And then there have always been the enormous hatreds borne by settlers out West. Ever since members of the class were born, those trying to make it in the country's Last West have been aggrieved. Choosing to head west as a result of financial panics, such as the one in 1873, or deciding to do so because they were restless or ambitious or couldn't make it anywhere else, they have gone out there in the millions. They've gone to pan for gold, drive cattle, plant wheat, lay track, herd sheep, survey sections, pull the teeth of whiskey-anesthetized cowboys in boomtowns, or to do thousands of other things. Many have dreamt of what is impossible in the Old World: the freely held farm, all their own. Many of them, lacking any source of timber on the prairie, have always built their damp but well-insulated sod houses— "soddies"—with thick prairie turf buttressed with stucco and plaster. By and large these westerners have always had a sod-size chip on their sweaty shoulders. And they've always had a couple of enemies: Indians and Easterners.

Four years before members of the class were born, the reck-less but heroic "Long Hair," General George Custer, as he sought "fresh laurels," led his blue-coated cavalry into total defeat in Montana. It was the Indians' last big win. Ever since—and for years before—the Indians have always lost. Over-matched by sheer numbers of palefaces with superior firepower, or subject to the white man's diseases, prey to the white man's liquor, betrayed by the white man's broken treaties, or devastated by the white man's shooting of essential buffalo for sport (even from railroad trains), they have largely been subdued. Their last big loss was in South Dakota when members of this class were ten; and their parents, who read the papers, have often said it must have had something to do with a "Ghost Dance" that had gotten out of hand.

As members of the class of 1898 have grown up, the solution seems to be the establishment of reservations, where Indians can be educated and civilized and instructed on how to make a living, mostly as farmers. They have never had any interest in the Christian tradition. They say they do not wish to quarrel about God as the white man does.

Nearly as much as Indians, Easterners have always been despised in the West. During the period of the West's settle-ment, which seems at an end now that class members are about to graduate from high school, it has always been guys with striped pants and silk ties who sit in big offices in New York, Boston, and Chicago who've done all sorts of nefarious things to little people. For sodbusters trying to get cheap land, East-erners have always defrauded the government land office and bought up huge swaths of the stuff and then sold it for a high price. For wheat farmers, some of them trying to "dry" farm, Easterners have always owned the railroads and managed to charge huge hauling prices. Or Easterners have made fun of Westerners when the latter went to the big Eastern cities, where they were called "hayseeds" who couldn't get used to sophisticated trends and unneighborly neighbors. It is Easterners who live high on the hog back in the filthy cities, such as Pittsburgh, where the air is so dirty that twilight always comes early.

It has always been Easterners who have used big money in order to bring barbed wire to the West, thus shutting off open access to the land. Easterners have taken away the romance of the grizzled gold prospectors, who, against long odds, tried to hit pay dirt with their picks and/or find it in their pans; or have erased the portrait of the cowboys, who, despite a life of loneliness, blizzards, rattlesnakes, and endless hours, have always been figures of gutsy sinew and grit. Expensive drill bits and "geological engineers" have always replaced the panhandlers, while cowboys are now more properly referred to as "ranch hands." A cowboy has never gotten rich; a cattleman almost never fails to do so.

Class members have grown up in a world where the legend and the transformation of the West have coexisted. But now in their eighteenth year, the matter is settled: the corporations have won. Mining and farming and ranching are now industries— just as they are back in the much-loathed East. The old cowboy in the West is as much stuck in the routines of the large ranch as is the Ukrainian immigrant stuck doing the same old thing every day, every hour, in the broiling steel mill back east.

* * * *

And yet, as class members are on the verge of graduating from high school, this mélange of mutual hatreds seems to be diminishing and turning into something else, something much more hopeful. As hatreds begin to wane ever so slightly, the other passion of the past eighteen years—confidence—has always seemed to wax. The undeniable facts seem to be that America is now an industrial producer on a par with Britain, Germany, and France and is the breadbasket not just for the rest of the country but also for fickle world markets. Railroads have improved—much heavier loads are now possible because of new technologies in braking. Thanks to railroads, Minneapolis has become the nation's flour merchant and Milwaukee the nation's brewer. New immigrants have had a desperate time adjusting to all sorts of new conditions—including challenges of the English language and fragmented factory work—but they also report that in America they don't have to tip their hats to the local land baron and that everything they enjoy is better here. "It is Sunday, and I have had my bath and milk," one immigrant has written to folks back home as he praised the paradise that, to him, is America. Immigrants, even if some returned home, have always helped to make America an industrial colossus. Maybe they will even become Americans rather than Slovaks or Macedonians who happen to be in America! After all, they're starting their school day with the Pledge of Allegiance now.

As for the West, it's over, isn't it? In 1890, the Census Bureau announced the end of the frontier. It's now a place of barbed wire, huge farms and ranches, machine-driven mining and farming, and rail lines everywhere. There's no need for a cowboy when the railroad can transport cattle much more easily and quickly; no need for a scythe when horse-drawn (thirty at a time) reapers and combines can cut the wheat in a tenth of the time; no need for a pan in a sluice when the gold can be drilled for. The great Wisconsin historian Frederick Jackson Turner has argued that the West has been a uniquely American promoter of cooperation and equality—that this stuff didn't all come to us from the Old World. Western folks gathering from miles around for quilting bees and hardy women in long calico skirts shooting bears and burning buffalo chips for fuel are unique to the American experience. But Professor Turner also says the West is done. Western farmers have organized to fight the railroads, the middlemen, and the bankers and to do battle with the gold standard and high tariffs; but when class members were sixteen, this populist revolt lost its last great battle in 1896, when William McKinley was elected president. The East had won.

No doubt the West itself will be forgotten by the next generation. The celebrations of it in dime novels about Bat Masterson and Bill Cody's Wild West shows with Annie Oakley and Sitting Bull should almost certainly become things of the past soon. Why, even primitive Dodge City has become what Huck Finn called "sivilized." In a decade, no one will care any longer about the boring old West.

The question of the freedmen has likewise become settled. The Negro hero of American whites has always been Booker T. Washington, who established an institute in Alabama for the professional training of black men to make a good living apart from whites. The Supreme Court has recently agreed wholeheartedly. Not many listen to another, more radical, black leader—William Edward Burghardt DuBois—who insists that if Negroes are to be fully American, they must also have exactly the same rights as the white man, even if it means an end to separation. This is almost certainly a pipe dream, and a dangerous one.

* * * *

Women, however, seem a tad more restless. Many of them still insist on closing saloons and on getting the vote—and out West, in places like Montana, they have already gotten it, at least on the state level. Thanks to the new industrialization, the development of new skills such as shorthand and bookkeeping, and new gadgets such as the typewriter, there's more demand for women's services in the big cities. Some of them have gone there by themselves and made and spent their own money. Legs have always been called limbs, but even so, some female members of the class of 1898 might wonder how much more independence might await them. The idea expressed by some feminist intellectuals that they might have the same strong sexual desires as men seems utterly far-fetched and much too daring. Riding bicycles, however, a delightful freedom, is growing more respectable all the time. Now women can don their "somewhat freer clothing" and join the "merry wheelmen" on their "wing'd steeds," now with equal wheel sizes for better balance.

The situation for class members who plan to become farmwives has always been quite different. They have darker expectations. A Department of Agriculture report from more than thirty years earlier remains valid today. It said that the farmer's wife is "a laboring drudge," and that the loneliness and work without end of farm life is, for her, an even heavier burden than that carried by her husband, who is at least free to chat with the hired hands and visit the local towns. Her jobs of making soap, butchering chickens, cooking meals, milking cows, washing clothes, and churning butter—not to mention other tasks such as spinning and hominy hulling—have led to farmwives being overrepresented in the local insane asylums. Though she needed to be hardy, she has been no less governed than were city women by the "Cult of True Womanhood," with its affirmation of piety, purity, domesticity, and submissiveness. These were qualities that may have led to an all-male jury's acquitting the infamous Lizzie Borden when class members were twelve, for no one could believe that any woman adherent of the Cult could bring down a hatchet on the brow of her sleeping father.

As for the boys in the class, eager to leave their stuffed and ornamented Victorian homes, they surely have a bright future. The nation is not at war and faces no immediate threat in that regard. To be sure, both Mrs. Jefferson Davis *and* Mrs. U. S. Grant say that the Spanish in Cuba fleece the virtue of fine women, and our battleship down there, say the Hearst papers, has been treacherously exploded by Spanish dynamite. Maybe we should do something about all that. But meanwhile, new industry means a comfortable new complexity. Young men who can read reports, add figures, and write memos are at a premium; and these high school graduates are just the ticket. They can easily imagine living in the big city, donning their coats and ties and inevitable derby hats, working as company managers, reading the new newspapers with their comic strips and garish lithographs, sneaking off to a burlesque show, or enjoying themselves at freak shows (where folks have always been deceived by "this way to the egress" signs, as though an egress were something like the Wild Man of Borneo).

They look forward to full participation in the passionate and entertaining battles between Republicans and Democrats, and they are aware that if their wives get the vote, it could lead to "ticket-splitting" in an era when anything less than united support for a single party has always been deemed unethical. These young men look forward to getting ahead and growing into full and "lusty manhood," complete with mustache and probably full beard—unlike William McKinley, the first president in years to be bare-faced. Should they be able to go to college, they might be free of the old, moribund subject of "moral philosophy," a loosely defined study of human nature and society that has now branched out into such useful specialties as economics and sociology. Higher education is changing: A teenager from the Deep South, class member Helen Keller, though blind and deaf, hopes to attend Radcliffe College. And Lucy Hayes, the former first lady, is actually a "college woman," something even more rare than a "college man."

If these young men join the millions now rushing into the big cities, they will first be living in a boardinghouse where they can eat like kings and live in comfort for four bucks a week. Thanks to the amazing new lightbulb, they can stay up later reading Mark Twain's *Pudd'nhead Wilson* or *The American Wheelman* magazine. At the very least they might become a salesman or a merchant, a senior clerk or an insurance man. They may have already read a popular new book by the Reverend Russell Conwell, who says that if you want acres of diamonds, dig in your own backyard. They must now feel confident that if they become industrious men, they will someday have a backyard—and a front yard *and* a horse and buggy—of their very own.

Rum
Has Always Been Demonic

Members of this class were born in 1900. If they finished high school, they would have done so around 1918. If they went to college (not likely), they would have finished in 1922.

Their classmates would have included Adlai Stevenson, Admiral Hyman Rickover, and Spencer Tracy.

Friedrich Nietzsche, Queen Victoria, President William McKinley, Oscar Wilde, and Sir Arthur Sullivan have always been dead.

Mindset List

1. Their baby pictures were probably taken at home on a Brownie box camera.

2. Thanks to Teddy Roosevelt, they've always thought "bully" was a good thing.

3. They've grown up with politicians advocating for national health care without success.

4. "Progressives" have always been concerned about urban slums, unfair monopolies, adulterated food, and "insufficiently chewed" food.

5. Lynching has always occurred throughout the country and has been routinely reported in newspapers almost on a weekly basis.

6. They've always known the United States as a world power that always wins its wars.

7. Millions of children have always worked six or seven days a week, for twelve hours or more for about twenty-five cents an hour.

8. Riding on an elevator has always been a thrill, second only to roller coasters.

9. The year they were born, for just a single greenback in small towns you could buy a peck of red apples, a scrub brush, three bars of soap, a can of oysters, a few dried prunes, *and* a tin of coffee.

10. Anarchists have always blown things up because people have taken away their freedoms.

11. They have always known one Roosevelt or another in national political life.

12. If they happened to miss church, they could always read about the sermons, which have always been considered news in Monday editions of big-city newspapers.

13. There have always been car shows, organized auto races, and transcontinental automobile tours.

14. During their childhood years stores were routinely converted to nickelodeons, becoming popular alternatives to vaudeville.

15. Their fathers might have tossed a few camphor balls in the gas tank in order to pep up the old Tin Lizzie.

16. With the creation of the American League, they've been able to visit grand baseball

parks, complete with a new area called the dugout.

17.   Young people have always changed their names to make them sound more American.

18.   They've always had the benefits of paper towels—and of regular toothbrushing, too.

19.   Rumor has always hinted that Coca-Cola contains cocaine.

20.   NBC has always meant the National Biscuit Company.

21.   The average top speed for automobiles has doubled from 20 miles per hour to a blinding 40.

22.   Gibson Girls have always worn shirtwaists, played golf, wowed men, and shocked their elders.

23.   A young lady's waist could never be too small.

24.   Hats have always been required attire except in bed.

25.   No one has ever known what to do with Alice Roosevelt.

26.   Their elders have always thought rouge or lipstick risqué.

27. Pipes, cigars, mustaches, and beards—but not
      cigarettes and wristwatches—have always
      been considered manly.

28. They're graduating from high school in a
      land where movies are just behind railroads,
      textiles, iron and steel, and oil as major
      national industries.

29. Swimming attire has always provided full
      coverage.

30. Their folks have always considered Corn
      Flakes, Grape Nuts, and Postum essential for
      good nutrition.

31. They've always enjoyed the Jell-O girl.

32. Big county fairs and amusement parks at
      the ends of trolley lines have always
      been an important part of summer
      entertainment.

33. Enrico Caruso has always offered His
      Master's Voice on scratchy Victor talking
      machines.

34. Tin Pan Alley, where the pianos never stop,
      has always existed on Twenty-eighth Street
      between Fifth Avenue and Broadway in New
      York City.

35. They've always read or heard about people going up in flying machines.

36. Their mothers still have their "St. Louis coat," which they bought at the World's Fair for an outrageous twenty-two dollars, and still recall doing the hoochie coochie and thrilling to the major Olympic event at the fair: the tug of war.

37. Sophie Tucker and W. C. Fields have always starred in burlesque and vaudeville but never in a "flicker."

38. They expect their parents to live into their fifties but few have known their grandparents for long, if at all.

39. For the fortunate few, holidays might have included an auto trip to the new national park at the Grand Canyon.

40. They will always remember when the phrase "I have the old Pole" made headlines everywhere.

41. The Temperance Movement has always been convinced that a great America must also be a booze-free one.

42. They have always bought ready-made clothes in their size off the rack.

43. Horseless carriages have always had steering wheels.

44. If fortunate, they've been able to read at night courtesy of incandescent lightbulbs.

45. The music most of them know best has always been beloved Protestant hymns.

46. The electric chair has always provided a humane alternative to hanging.

47. Someone has always been selling—or investigating—patent medicines, and snake oil has always provided a cure for everything; you're promised a cash reward if you're not cured.

48. Horse-drawn streetcars have always been so very 1870s.

49. Babe Ruth, pitching for the Red Sox, has never hit more than eleven home runs in a year, but is hoping someday to break the record of twenty-four held by Frank "Home Run" Baker.

50. San Franciscans have always feared another big earthquake.

* * * *

In the first decade of the twentieth century the prosperous Tates of 504 East Seventh in Charlotte, North Carolina, posed for a family portrait. In this austere photograph they sit unsmiling, with the women in typical high collars and long skirts, the men in formal suits and ties, and some of the kids in sailor suits, then fashionable. It is an extremely formal image, but not abnormally so by the standards of the time. Even the children are earnest, for the age took its cue from Henry Wadsworth Longfellow's declaration half a century earlier that "Life is real! Life is earnest! And the grave is not its goal." Beneath the expressions of gravity was a sense of determination and pride, for the twentieth century began with the United States having achieved the status of the world's number one industrial power. Even the Tates, whose South was by far the least industrialized part of the land, seemed by their demeanors to take part in a general feeling that America the Ever Wholesome was superior to Europe the Increasingly Decadent. The disastrous Civil War of about forty years ago, which so shattered the confidence of the nation in its institutions and its prospects, by now seems long ago and far away, and Americans' faith in their future has been thoroughly restored. Yet, as the Tates suggested by their pious and serious mien, this is not a time to celebrate such success prematurely. Indeed, as the Tate children grow to maturity, they will experience a strong and stern sobriety—though within twenty years of the time this portrait was made, such Puritanism will encounter, for an outrageous little while, flapping and frivolous opposition in a decade that veritably roared.

* * * *

The high school graduates of the class of 1918 are a lucky bunch. Though it isn't likely they'll also go on to college (or play football for those premier teams at Harvard and Yale), if they do, they might become doctors, lawyers, bankers, businessmen, or teachers, the latter especially proper for the girls. With a high school diploma they can become clerks, tellers, managers, or shop owners. Everyone else their age will toil in the countryside picking cotton or mining coal at the edge of town or toting steel bars in the city or sewing garments or slaughtering cattle. Mine owners and steel magnates have never let their factory workers get away with working fewer than twelve hours a day, and Sunday was their only day off. The number of American youngsters killed or maimed in accidents on the job has exceeded the number that graduate from college.

Though members of the class are aware of their good fortune in being able to get a high school education, they've always known at least a few people who could hardly read or write. These might have been new immigrants in the cities— Italians or Poles, for instance—or more likely native-born "country folks," who attended school only sporadically if at all. They were sharecropper kids, who hoped for good markets, decent soil, cooperative weather, and fair landlords. Their families had none of those newfangled steam tractors. Their idea of gold was a good mule. Lamp oil was costly to them and their families. They've always lived dawn to dusk and probably always will. Those who graduated from high school in 1918 have had evenings after nine in the summer and after five in the winter when they could read *The Red Badge of Courage* or *Ladies' Home Journal*—another sign of their good luck. Yet even in towns of several thousand, where electric lighting has become the rule, it has always been common for folks to still keep horses, cows, and pigs in their backyards.

These students have grown up in an America where railroads have greatly diminished the importance of river transports. Places like Hannibal, Missouri, and Paducah, Kentucky, once bustling with commerce and river traffic, are now much reduced. The number of Americans working on farms is still higher than the number working in factories, but the latter are fast closing the gap. When they were born, the geographical center of the United States had, in one hundred years, moved 475 miles west and is now in Columbus, Indiana, in what was called, just fifty years earlier, "the West." When they were still in diapers, the country had fewer than two hundred miles of paved roads.

Their parents were worried that their infants would catch diphtheria, typhoid, or malaria. They've grown up being spanked for even whispering in church, and no rod was ever spared on them. Though the most fortunate among them have had store-bought toys, many of them have made do quite nicely with blocks, kites, and stilts. Their older brothers have always been tempted to smoke by the baseball cards included in cigarette packs, and as they themselves have grown up, they've often found the spare Wee Willie Keeler or Nap Lajoie card about the house. Mischievous Buster Brown and his wise if sardonic dog Tige have both entertained and instructed them in the "funny papers" about avoiding such errors in judgment as showing kindness to trifling tramps.

If they have gone to a rural school, they will have learned a lot from the time-honored *McGuffey's Reader*, from which they've gotten a generous helping of good verse, moral tales, and spelling rules. None of the males in the class would have passed

up a Frank Merriwell dime novel, because Frank, a student at
Yale, is ever handsome, muscular, athletic, kind, honest, and
resourceful. He has won races against rival Harvard and beaten
Chinese land pirates and city gangs. A good sport, he has always
hated booze and bullies. The boys in the class of '18 have
grown up wanting to be just like Frank.

"In the Good Old Summertime" has always been one of
the most beloved songs in the United States, and the season has
always been one of cherished "swimming cricks," parades, and
baseball. For the better-off it has always meant summer resorts
at the shore or in the mountains. By the time they were six,
there were over a hundred circus troupes traveling around the
land, featuring lions, tigers, elephants, trapeze artists, clowns,
ringmasters, and bearded ladies for the entertainment of "boys
and girls and men and women of all ages."

Their childhood and adolescence have always been dominated by a single great figure: Teddy Roosevelt. Teddy has made
them more likely to take chances and exercise strenuously.
Teddy has encouraged the males in the class to be perpetual
boys. As someone once said, "The president is about six." At the
same time he has always worried about the important things,
and he once established a commission to investigate the decline
of the virtuous American small town. As children they may
have slept with their Teddy Bears; in fact, their parents might
have taken a photo of them and Teddy with a new Brownie box
camera. They weren't all that old when he officially left the scene
as president, about the time his cousin Franklin Delano Roosevelt became assistant secretary of the navy, but Teddy, well, he's
always been around. Teddy sent the U.S. Navy around the world,
and under Teddy the United States has become a world power,
complete with its own colonies in Cuba and the Philippines.

Teddy gave the word "bully" a positive spin, whatever the Filipinos may have thought about it.

Those who came after him, such as William Howard Taft, have always seemed to be from an earlier time. Taft was portly and sedentary and so very 1880s. Woodrow Wilson has always seemed a bit sissy, without even a mustache. After the Germans began sinking our merchant ships, their parents may have commented that Wilson's mantra "Too proud to fight" was on the cowardly side.

The lads in the class of '18 have always wanted to look older and more mature as they grew up. For the most part they've been able to assume that men were men, and that women were glad of it. They've wanted to grow mustaches or beards because being barefaced has always seemed effeminate. So is smoking cigarettes, so the men prefer to smoke cigars or pipes. Like their fathers, they will wear hats everywhere but in the house and at formal sit-down occasions such as church services. Ties have always been required even for baseball games on blistering summer days, though you were permitted to skip the flannel coat part if it was really hot. A home run, though exceedingly rare, might have even made them forget how uncomfortable they were. Women have always been urged to wear padded layers and endless numbers of ruffles, and, like the men, have always worn hats everywhere. If men have always had their bowlers, then the women have always had the milky-white feathers of egrets and herons to serve as their own crowns (no matter what the Audubon Society might think). Men had their spats, while the ladies had their iron-reinforced corsets.

Father has always been the boys' masculine ideal. Although he may only live to be about fifty, he is a paragon of manly virtue, complete with his silver cane, silver glasses case, pocket watch, bowler hat, and collar and cuffs (both detachable). With his leather strop he keeps his straight razor sharp, and with his shaving mug the soap always lathers ferociously. And there is the pomade for his mustache. He craves the pleasures that only a man can enjoy, and this especially includes a good fifteen-cent shave at the barber shop, also an outpost of bully talk. He may very well be a member of a club, maybe an exclusive one, and has probably joined the local volunteer fire company, which spends part of its time racing against other fire companies in summer contests. He has always taught them to admire men like the bushy-bearded explorer Robert Peary, who in 1909, reported, truthfully, "I have the old Pole," when he first stomped his furred boot inside the Arctic Circle.

But if Father's and Teddy's manly formality has always been the ideal for the boys, then the Gibson Girl has been the rather subversive model for the girls of the class, who have grown up thinking that, like the Gibson Girl, they too could wear the more casual shirtwaist (blouse) and skirt instead of a dress, that they too could bike and play tennis (and maybe even vote some-day?), and that they too could become social workers or phone operators. At least they might mime the Gibson Girl's eyes—at once artfully distant and indifferent but also keenly intelligent. They can aspire to take the "Gibson Cure" and acquire that lean, dignified look that drives the boys mad. This is not to suggest, of course, that a woman's place is not principally in the home and always shall be. Getting the vote might be nice, however, and so would getting to do what Mother has done: join a charitable or self-improvement club. Maybe they will move to a city and become one of those "lady typewriters" and meet a charismatic and handsome young suitor as well, as portrayed in the romance magazines. He could be one of the clerks.

* * * *

Those of the class of 1918 smart enough to finish high school and get a job also got to visit nickelodeons, where pictures shuttered noisily and moved along for up to fifteen or twenty minutes. No nickel was ever better spent. They could drool over Theda Bara, her name appropriately an anagram of "Arab death." Father and Mother might object, but few things have ever been more enticing than an unsmiling and exotic vamp. The old vaudevillians, though, don't think much of nickelodeons—they despise the competition, especially now that the expanding "movie" industry has moved to Southern California, where you can "shoot" year-round, in order to escape an Eastern monopoly.

By the time they were teens, nickelodeons were competing with vaudeville by featuring "scenics," "actualities," comedies, and even boxing matches, with organ or piano music to match (always expect ragtime for chase scenes). They could view a mountain valley from a moving train, see how a train engine was made, or watch Jack Johnson knock silly the latest candidate for Great White Hope. Many people think Johnson is a bestial savage, little better than a white slaver, but whatever public opinion about that may be, they have to admit that the man can brawl like no other fighter can.

Player pianos have always played ragtime, and sometimes the town's best pianist (outside church) might even get the sheet music and play it himself at a local saloon and hope that old Mrs. Schofield down at the First Methodist Sunday School, with her gossipy tongue, never found out—because she has long been saying that there's a plot to drown out hymns with ragtime and flood America the Beautiful in whiskey and gin.

Ragtime (like the jazz that's maybe starting to become even more popular) could be a little on the side of the devil's music, but just as with Jack Johnson and his boxing, members of this class have always acknowledged that these colored musicians can certainly get their feet tapping.

Their older brothers have always told them about heading to a saloon and listening to the piano player rap out "Maple Leaf Rag" and hearing some great Irish jokes, as when Mr. Lodge asked Paddy what Mike had died of, and Paddy replied that "he died of a Tuesday." With all due respect to the Irish Catholics, some Protestant members of the class of '18 have conceded that the Irish are real Americans, but your citified Irish have always seemed to be a different sort of American: too loud, too drunk, too sentimental, too glib. One class member, however, a young man named Spencer Tracy, graduated from a Catholic high school in Milwaukee and is now attending a Protestant college where he is starting to develop an interest in stage acting—unusual.

As for colored people, members of the class have always heard about lynching, even in the North, and some have seen them or even taken part. While these incidents have occurred with frequency, they've never been big news. W. E. B. DuBois, a Negro leader, has written that his people sometimes wonder whether they should consider themselves to be Negroes first or Americans. Booker T. Washington, long admired by their parents, has always insisted that colored people should be Americans before all else. One reason nickelodeons are dying out is that *Birth of a Nation*, the film that celebrated the Ku Klux Klan for restoring honest government to the South and delivering it from a venal federal administration, has made the old shorts seem pointless and insignificant, but has also led to several riots and even to a murder, by a white man of a colored man, in central Indiana. Along with the film's great new close-up and fade-out shots have come a measure of violence and death. Woodrow Wilson got a private screening in the White House and was thrilled, saying it was like writing history "with lightning" and was so "terribly true."

* * * *

Their grandparents, barely remembered if at all, had always done everything for themselves, and that included oiling their own lamps and chopping their own wood. They always made their own clothes. But now you can get clothes made in your size, and you can buy them off the rack. Especially if they grew up in the cities, the class of 1918 has always been aware of some various commercial enterprises warming and lighting their homes and putting shirts on their backs. Their parents may have had coal delivered from a company the next town over, in order to heat steam radiators that some faraway firm had manufactured; or their parents may have even had electricity wired into their home for Mr. Thomas Edison's lightbulbs. General Electric patented these bulbs when class members were only six. Yet the rural areas, where most still live, remain left behind, still heating homes with fireplaces or Franklin stoves and reading by oil lamps.

They've grown up with the greatest wish book ever published: the Sears, Roebuck catalog, from which Mother and Father could order heating stoves, talking machines, bust cream, toilet sets, teapots, patent medicines, curling irons, and thousands of other "sundries."

When they were in their teens, their parents could buy a Victor Talking Machine and hear Enrico Caruso himself, from faraway Italy, hitting the high notes of "O Sole Mio." It has always sounded a little scratchy, but it was a lot better than not having Caruso at all.

They've attended church—mostly small ones—all their lives. Even towns of only two or three thousand people have always had—and always will have—at least one Methodist, Baptist, Presbyterian, Lutheran, Congregational, and Episcopal church. Only the big cities have big churches. Although they've been familiar with other types of music—including ragtime and Sousa marches and Strauss waltzes and dear old songs like "Dearie"—the music they know best has always been Protestant hymns. They have always known the tune of "O Worship the King" at least as well as they know the "Stars and Stripes Forever" or anything written by Victor Herbert. The *New York Times* has always provided on Mondays the text of sermons in the city from the previous day.

There have always been other forms of entertainment, such as county fairs, local dances (if the church permitted), nickelodeons (in bigger places, of course), family reunions, and trolley parks at the ends of the trolley tracks like Coney Island. There have always been dancers, singers, magicians, jugglers, farces, and melodramas down at the local "opera house." Church has always been the center of family life outside the home. Otherwise family life is focused on shared meals at dinnertime or just sitting on the porch or by the fire talking. If Mother or Sister could play piano, so much the better, for most live music has always been in the home, with "Home Sweet Home" and "Columbia, the Gem of the Ocean" as special family favorites.

* * * *

But the saloons have never gone away, and there has always been a strong movement to outlaw them and forbid forever the satanic spirits they continue to offer. A few voices have said that drinking is a public health issue, but all their lives the class of 1918 has heard the argument that it's a moral issue. Members of the temperance movement have always entered saloons in order to urge, by singing and prayer, that they close. As students, the members of this class have been immersed in the movement's teachings, since every state has mandated that several hours a week be devoted to Scientific Temperance Instruction, and in some states the birthday of Women's Christian Temperance Union founder Frances Willard was even observed with a school holiday.

And as they've grown up, what used to be a movement has become a legislative agenda, now demanding the outright prohibition of the sale and consumption of alcoholic beverages. A constitutional amendment now seems inevitable. A majority, it seems, are convinced that this will make the United States a far better place, for "Drys" cite not only the evils of drink but also all the ills linked with it, such as prostitution and divorce. Temperance has always been the major topic of Sunday sermons. Their grandparents, many of whom fought in the Civil War, have often told them that temperance has replaced slavery as the leading moral issue of the day. And they can believe it. It took a constitutional amendment or two to settle the slavery issue, too.

The folks who favor temperance haven't just been asking whether you're for or against the demon rum. They've also wondered whether all these immigrants coming to America at the pace of about a million a year should really be here; what kinds of drinking habits they have; what sorts of religious heritage they bring (likely Catholic or Jewish or, well, anything but Protestant); whether it's a good idea for them to be living in Polish or Jewish hovels and enclaves in crowded and filthy cities; and whether they're taking jobs from real Americans. Already at least one immigrant, Hyman Rickover, a Russian Jew, has just graduated from a Chicago high school. Members of the class of '18 have heard their parents ask: Will these people change us, or will we change them?

True, the big cities have always been growing and growing, but most Americans have always lived outside them and probably always will. The difference between New York City and Marion, Ohio, seems to be so great that members of the class of 1918 might well wonder if the two are even in the same country. In Marion you would hardly ever see a strange face, while in New York you hardly ever see a familiar one. In Marion you can see all sorts of interesting things just by keeping your eyes steady and looking across the way. In New York, however, you often have to look upward just to see the sky; the good citizens of Marion have always wondered why New Yorkers don't have cricks in their necks. At least they've heard that New York is improving: without all the clop-clopping of horses on the streets, you can hear the person next to you, and without all the blowing manure, you can smell something pleasant every now and then.

* * * *

If class members were prosperous enough to get to finish high school, then they have probably been able to ride on the passenger trains that have always crisscrossed the country. Folks who live in towns near the cities—they've heard the term "suburbs" being used more and more—have always been able to walk to the station, commute to the city, and then return home in the evening. It's never been uncommon to take the train from coast to coast on a Pullman Palace Sleeper Car, and many small towns have prospered by becoming railroad terminals and setting up small hotels.

As for the horseless carriage, well, it's always been just that, a carriage. Few of them have ever been wholly enclosed vehicles. You always left your goggles behind at your own risk. Steam and electricity have fallen behind internal combustion as the way to run those things, but the young people have heard many stories about how unreliable they are. Although the new steering wheels seem to be helping a lot, when they were younger, a lot of the carriages were moved around by tillers. They had only one speed, were the devil to start, and often broke down, and people often remarked that a horse wouldn't do that. Automobiles have continued to get better, though, and lots of them now have suspensions and more than one speed. Some now even start from inside the carriage, so you don't have to crank them outside. The number being produced now, compared to the year they were born, is over one hundred times greater, so they aren't just for hobbyists any longer. Henry Ford's Model T (or "Tin Lizzie" or "flivver") is becoming a common sight. They say she can sometimes do up to 40 miles per hour.

When this class was very young, autos were mainly the playthings of the very rich, who could afford $4,500 to buy a Pierce "Great Arrow" touring car and could easily spend twenty-five bucks at Hammacher Schlemmer on such necessary accessories as towing cable, an extra fan belt, wrenches, gauges, screwdrivers, and several-pound packages of "hardtack." They could buy the special long-flowing "motoring gowns," too. Horses all over the United States were getting a rest and were being born in fewer numbers. Some were slaughtered, as they were now considered expensive to maintain and no longer necessary.

Almost no one in the class has ever been up in an airplane, which has now sparked controversy as a weapon of war; but they may well know the words to "Take Me Up with You, Dearie." These flying machines are considered "contraptions" if ever there were any: enormous, bulky, complex, and more apt to fail than not. But if the "Silver Darts" and "quintaplanes" didn't always fly, the gas-filled dirigible generally did, and when they were eight it became the army's first ever airship. Now that the members of this class are graduating from high school, of course, the "aeroplane" has played a military role in the Great War. Some go so far as to say that it will be *the* weapon of the future.

The cities and larger towns have always had telephone switchboard exchanges, and they've always provided jobs to the operators who are necessary to run them. The "earpiece," cradle, and ringer box have commonly been separate, and sometimes they've worked only from one person's phone to another person's phone, or they've had to be shared on a party line with the attendant temptation to listen in on a neighbor's conversation. But they've been getting better, and a few lucky people have always been able to talk coast to coast. There's even talk that someday you won't have to pick up the phone and hear some woman say "Number, please" in order to get your party.

* * * *

Besides Teddy Roosevelt, the political phenomenon they've grown up with has been the Progressive Movement. The Progressives have always been obsessed with the long and grueling hours worked by men, women, and children in the big factories and with the evils of indirect democracy, adulterated bacon, poor education, inherited ignorance, feeblemindedness, and pervasive dirt (class members have grown up in school having their fingernails inspected by humorless schoolmarms). One well-known Progressive has a mortal fear of inadequately chewed food and argues for consumption of fruit and vegetable juice only. He and other Progressives have always supported the direct election of U.S. senators, government oversight in the preparation of commercial foodstuffs, and better and more universal education. They've always liked the clean outdoors and adored the idea of big national parks in the West, where the air is pure and the scenery is as pristine as it is spectacular. One Progressive, the journalist Ida Tarbell, so annoyed John D. Rockefeller with her revelations of corporate skullduggery that he dubbed her "Ida the Turrabel."

If Teddy and the Progressives have been the dominating political figures of their time, the dominating political forces of their time have been the lethal threats of anarchists and the rise of the Great War. Anarchists have always declared war on those who would take away their freedoms. They have always come in many forms—from collectivist to capitalist, from individualistic to socialist—but their underlying idea has always been the same: any restraint imposed by one human on another is wrong. Somehow, anarchists have always reasoned, if we get rid of that restraint, everything will be fine.

This has always seemed vague and utopian, but the anarchists, armed with recent access to plenty of dynamite, have always meant business. When class members were in their prams, an anarchist murdered one American president, and during the childhood and teens of this class anarchists managed to blow up several important structures, including the *Los Angeles Times* building. It's always seemed a mighty funny way to end the evils of restraint. Their parents say it's high time the government cracked down so that these radical ideas will be expunged once and for all. One anarchist, Red Emma Goldman, observed that the crank who killed President McKinley was "a man with the beautiful soul of a child." Where will anarchists strike next—Wall Street?

When the Great War erupted far away, they were fourteen. Everyone was shocked that such butchery could be triggered by the assassination of an obscure aristocrat in a remote part of the world. Their parents and grandparents observed that that was Europe for you. The crowned heads were vain, and the whole continent reeked of mutual distrust and deadly armaments.

By the time President Wilson did get us into the war—in 1917, when it seemed that we just couldn't take this unrestricted submarine warfare any longer or tolerate the Huns' conspiring with Mexico against us—members of the class of 1918 were a tad too young to be drafted. It now seems the war might be over soon. One of their number, Adlai Stevenson, from a prominent Illinois family, has volunteered, but it's not clear that he'll ever see action before the conflict ends. Meanwhile, especially if they grew up in smaller towns, people named Lehrmann or Linnenberg or Fritz (no matter if they were good Lutherans) were objects of whispering suspicion, even if no one ever said anything directly to the families. Others of the Hun persuasion were less lucky and got fired or tarred and feathered, or even lynched in one town in southern Illinois. "German" measles are now "liberty" measles, and "dachshunds" are now "liberty pups." In the view of most Americans, the Hun is completely uncivilized. He has always pillaged and raped. But maybe he'll soon be whipped.

* * * *

Most of the class of 1918 managed to avoid the war, and members of the class, as they are contemplating the rest of their lives, have always been able to feel good about their general health. People are living longer. Indoor plumbing is becoming much more common. Steam heat is a lot cleaner than heat from Franklin stoves. Certain deadly diseases, such as malaria and yellow fever, which were widespread in other parts of the world, have now been almost wiped out. A vaccine for typhoid has always been available, and the medicine clearly works. Infant mortality is too high, say the Progressives, and far too many in the class of 1918 have lost their mothers in childbirth; but hookworm, discovered to be a terrible threat, is now being eradicated. Barring an outbreak of something like severe influenza, members of the class have reason to feel good about their longevity. They wouldn't be surprised if even their forty-year-old parents lived into their fifties or even a bit longer.

All this optimism notwithstanding, at a time when doctors have posted their prices on the walls of their offices (getting a broken leg set might set you back a buck), they've always grown up with patent medicines. To be sure, those who hawk them— mainly traveling by horse-drawn wagons from town to town—

have been called snake oil salesmen. But these concoctions always been hailed as universal cures, and they've included some pretty colorful elixirs, such as Lydia Pinkham's herbal pills and Kickapoo Indian "Sagwa." These would supposedly cure everything from hoarseness to gout, and increase vitality and strength—attributes Teddy Roosevelt would admire. The best way to embrace the "muscular Christianity" that has always been part of their lives is to love Christ and train hard. But Charles Stanley's liniment might help, too, at least for sore muscles, even if the government has analyzed the stuff and said it contains red pepper and turpentine and a lot of other questionable stuff. It was rumored that some of these elixirs have often included alcohol and even cocaine in high proportions (a rumor that also plagued Coca-Cola). Moving the bowels has always been a national obsession, it seems, and there's always been senna for that.

Father says that their late grandmother had always taken something off the medicine wagon to calm her nerves. When they were six, the Bureau of Chemistry, later to be called the Food and Drug Administration, started to crack down on these alleged charlatans, while others insisted that it was none of the government's business. After all, some doctors have prescribed this stuff, and if people want to go to quacks, that should be their business. The class of 1918 has always loved that old pun about phony claims: "We've heard ducks like that quack before."

As the class of 1918 looks ahead, they have reason to feel optimistic. Surely no war in their lifetime will ever approach the horrors of this one with its trench warfare and poison gas and ridiculously high casualties. Doctors will someday eradicate flu just as they have stamped out typhoid and malaria. One thing seems certain: this country is booming, and it will always be rich, righteous, and ready for anything. Who knows? Old Teddy himself might be president again by 1921. Why not? At last everything will go back to how it was, or at least to how it's supposed to be.

They've Always Been Spoiled by Zippers

B orn in 1913, fewer than a third of the members of this class would have completed elementary school, and fewer than 10 percent would have graduated from high school as the Great Depression began to stifle the economy. If they had been part of the extremely privileged group to make it all the way through college, they would have joined the class of '35. During these first thirty years of the twentieth century, the majority of American kids had little childhood at all.

Members of their class include Richard Nixon, Rosa Parks (born Rosa Louise McCauley), and Mary Martin.

For them, Harriet Tubman, J. P. Morgan, and Adolphus Busch have always been dead.

Mindset List

1. Every business that is anything at all has a typewriter.

2. New York's Long Island has always beckoned to those who want a house in the country.

3. The night they were born, Father may have distracted himself with a *New York Herald* crossword puzzle while savoring a Camel cigarette.

4. Americans have always complained about having to pay income tax.

5. There has never really been a *Titanic*, although they grew up hearing stories about its tragic journey.

6. Songs like "Danny Boy" and "Mother Machree" have always brought a tear to Father's eye.

7. Europe has always been a decadent and barbaric place of political assassinations, ancient grudges, swarthy immigrants, and even a "classical music riot" in Paris during the premiere of Igor Stravinsky's offbeat ballet "Rite of Spring."

8. Until their senior year in high school, New York City was able to claim the Woolworth Building as the tallest in the United States.

9. Henri Matisse, Marcel Duchamp, and Igor Stravinsky have always been pushing people over the edge.

10. The forward pass has always been a way to advance the football.

11. Broadcasting has always had more to do with sound waves than with spreading seed on the farm.

12. People have always questioned the health benefits of daily baths.

13. Erector Sets have always been the toy of choice for budding engineers.

14. They, however infrequently, have always been able to make telephone calls across the country.

15. Pyrex has always been able to go in the oven.

16. New York has always aspired to become the fashion capital of the world.

17. You can get your dental work done at Bloomingdale's.

18. In the wake of the Triangle Shirtwaist fire tragedy two years before they were born, old theaters and tenements have been shut down to comply with strict new fire codes.

19. It has never been legal to transport dynamite during the day in lower Manhattan.

20. Phone companies have always been trying to educate their customers not to employ profane language on the instrument, and users who persist in doing so have seen their service cut off.

21. Drivers have always been able to start cars without cranking them.

22. Ragtime dances like the Turkey Trot and the Bunny Hug have never been performed in proper company.

23. Despite the White-Slave Traffic (or Mann) Act, prohibiting the abduction of women for employment as prostitutes, panicky rumors of white slavery have continued to recur.

24. They are relieved that tuberculosis—aka "consumption"—seems to be on the way to being wiped out.

25.   City mansions have continued to fall under the onslaught of retailers and expanding downtown shopping areas.

26.   It seems that everybody has always taken the train to Detroit in order to build vehicles that are starting to replace the train.

27.   Father's money has always been affected by Federal Reserve Banks.

28.   They've always heard that the country can't build roads fast enough.

29.   Once they are eligible to vote in 1934, they'll be able to elect their U.S. senators directly, thanks to ratification of the Seventeenth Amendment.

30.   Tarzan has always thrilled them by swinging in jungle trees and beating his bare chest, first in books and then on the movie screen.

31.   Passenger pigeons have always been extinct.

32.   Respectable girls have always "petted."

33.   For their parents the cocktail party is the new new thing.

34.   The tomboy look for women is becoming more fashionable.

35. The state of Utah has long disapproved of skirts higher than three inches above the ankle.

36. Their parents were among the first to get on the installment plan when making a major purchase.

37. As they were starting junior high, Jesus Christ himself was hailed as a mass-marketing genius who stressed "great service."

38. Their parents have routinely sought advice from experts on how to raise them.

39. Jazz musicians and the Ku Klux Klan have always been out in front in the race for the most preposterous vocabulary.

40. The divorce rate has been climbing; nearly one in five marriages now ends in divorce.

41. Sports heroes have always been national, not local.

42. They've grown up as Boy Scouts and Campfire Girls, learning how to be square and how to build fires by rubbing two sticks together.

43. Summer camping has always meant a stop at Abercrombie's Camp Store.

44. Father has always kept the windows open for better radio reception.

45. People have always been able to get a ride in a taxicab but some are still unsure about how much to tip.

46. Courtesy of wireless radio waves, class members have always been able to rest more assured about railroad safety.

47. There has always been a special day to celebrate Mother.

48. During their relatively brief lifetimes, Herbert Hoover has gone from an international hero to a national villain.

49. While they were still toddlers, their mothers, aunts, and older sisters did the war work of repairing autos, delivering telegrams, and operating streetcars in order to help make the world safe for democracy.

50. They fell asleep on their parents' laps as Indians danced "The Mating of the Eagle" and speakers urged self-improvement at the local Tent Chautauqua.

* * * *

In 1920 a photographer snapped a photo of a boy, about seven, who might well have been a member of the class of 1931. He is looking at a movie billboard of The Mollycoddle, *a silent film comedy with Douglas Fairbanks Sr. starring as Richard Marshall V, an American who has spent most of his life playing polo and wearing a monocle in Europe. His American mettle is tested when he hooks up with a duplicitous gang of diamond thieves on their way to Arizona. This is also a snapshot of the class of 1931, whose parents grew up when the Old West was much more real and current. Now updated, the West is a popular theme for the new miracle technology, the "movies," and this one celebrates instinctive American bravery at the expense of the stuffed-shirt Europeans that the country's doughboys had so recently bailed out overseas. The little boy in the photograph stands at the threshold of the 1920s, when the country would turn inward to the new mass consumption, the new time-saving conveniences, and the new entertainment technologies. Little does he know that within just eleven years he and other young Americans will be called upon by economic calamity to be as brave and resourceful as Richard Marshall V.*

* * * *

For the high school class of 1931 it has been eighteen years of fear and distrust, hope and expectation, promise and disappointment. It has been a time of new experiences, expansion, and creativity as cars fill the streets, top average speeds rise to 50 miles per hour, and motorized vehicles regularly run over people. When he was president of Princeton, Woodrow Wilson declared that such driving arrogance by the upper crust was leading to a dangerous increase in "socialistic feeling" on the part of the working class. Inventions have simplified everyday chores and enhanced communication both within communities and throughout the nation. The growth of a consumer culture has offered a vision of the good life. It's been a time of lost innocence about those cynical and murderous Europeans, of growing artistic ferment, and of promoting the self-indulgence that comes with widespread prosperity. The moral fabric has frayed, though there have still been plenty of Puritans in Babylon, as someone once referred to prim old Cal Coolidge. And now it's all ending with a big and hideous crash. When the class of '31 were five, Herbert Hoover fed the world and was seen as a national and international savior. Now that they are eighteen, he is the national scapegoat, a dark and atrocious one. He doesn't know what to do, and it's obvious to everyone.

Regardless of the economy, everything has begun to move more quickly, with larger ships, faster trains, and a shortened route between the Atlantic and Pacific oceans. Airmail and transcontinental phone lines help people to keep in touch with the folks back home in the Midwest and elsewhere. Parcel shipping is as close as the local post office. Class members' elders have always complained that the world is moving too fast. Even getting dressed has gotten easier with the popular new zipper, despite the occasional defective device leaving a person half-dressed for the long walk home from school. Even so, won't these convenient new zippers be apt to spoil them? They don't even have to bother buttoning their coats now!

Train stations like the monumental new Grand Central Terminal of New York City—a symbol of the vile urban setting condemned by the KKK, Prohibitionists, and William Jennings Bryan in his search for the common folk—provide a dramatic setting for beginning new lives. People who had once turned their backs on rural America or the old country are now, a generation later, embracing the openness of the newly accessible suburbs. Developers are offering the adjacent countryside as an opportunity to live like landed gentry in a manor house. One of them, a fictional character named Jay Gatsby who lives regally out on East Egg, Long Island, has until recently been a self-invented symbol of the Good Life, 1920s style. This was before the crash, and since then life has become bad, maybe forever. The fast-living Gatsby has apparently gone the way of old autos with steering tillers.

But if some autos were old, the class members themselves were decidedly young and new. There was about a 30 percent chance that they were born in a hospital, and about a 50/50 chance that a physician attended their births. If they were born in the hospital, Father and Mother might have brought them home in the new Maxwell, for the automobile was completing the transition from its former status as a luxury, hobby, or novelty item. More than a score of car manufacturers have been working to attract the folks' attention and buying power. With more than a million cars on the road—a quarter of them purchased the year before this class was born—the United States has become the world's center for car production. Places like Daytona and Indianapolis are already identified internationally with speed and entertainment.

As these kids have become older teenagers, cars have provided them with a new freedom to socialize and get away from the folks and their Victorian supervision. Parents may have been among the thousands around the country who contributed a day for roadwork to help build the Lincoln Highway from coast to coast. Class members have never seen a horse-drawn trolley, but they have seen cars that start with a button from inside. They have also seen drivers, who must now be licensed, pulled over by police for speeding or intoxication or failing to obey one of the newly installed traffic lights. Their parents' Model T had over a hundred parts, including an attachment for generating electricity and plowing fields and a frame so sturdy "she" could stand just about anything. Its price, with mass production, continued to drop until Mr. Ford replaced it, when they were thirteen, with the new Model A.

But access to travel represents more than the chance to enjoy family excursions. Before they were born, the president of the United States had already made his way to Panama to confirm the progress being made on the Panama Canal. With that, Teddy Roosevelt started the practice of presidents leaving the country to celebrate their accomplishments. Then, when they were about five, Woodrow Wilson went to Versailles with a proposal that had four points more than God had commandments. He was gone so long that some began to worry that this would set a precedent of presidents traveling abroad to affirm their achievements while also escaping domestic criticism. While diplomatic in tone, such trips have always been prompted by the growing need to protect the "dignity and authority" of the United States, thereby strengthening the growing international business and political interests of the United States.

* * * *

"Trust" has always been a roller-coaster principle for this generation. It has been hard to know whom to trust or whom to believe as they have grown and government has grown right along with them. When they were small, muckraker Upton Sinclair was writing about the poisonous conditions of slaughterhouses, which made everyone squeamish about eating beef. Everybody has a relative or a neighbor who has been carried away by the swine flu or as a result of a distant war involving strange national figures, like thickly mustachioed Turkish soldiers with their gold-plated helmets topped by mosquelike spires. These odd-looking people surely had nothing to do with us until we were suddenly in the midst of the conflict. Once the war to end all wars was over, with over a hundred thousand of our men slaughtered, seemingly unimportant world leaders, like Ho Chi Minh of Indochina, tried to get in to see President Wilson.

Wars for their parents and grandparents had been relatively quiet, small, formal affairs incurred to protect our interests and our borders. Really big wars had always been someone else's business. Warfare abroad had not changed its form in a century. Soldiers from ancient empires used to march in fine uniforms and precise ranks into direct combat, taking time off on holidays. Aging immigrant relatives or servants explained to class members the horrible conflicts in Europe during their own younger years, with the caveat that these ancient rivalries and the perverse sport of war were among the forces that drove these aged kinfolk or maids to seek a life in the New World. This country should have nothing to do with such struggles, they've always said, for this is why they left Europe in the first place.

Outside of these cautionary stories and family losses, class members themselves have been spared the experience of the Great War. The ugly new form of warfare and the deadly scale of the new mechanized weapons would touch them only later as they went to school and learned European geography without Austro-Hungarian and Turkish empires found anywhere on the map. Thank God there will never be another war like this one, they think. Their parents must have been overjoyed that their little ones were too young to have perished in the Great War, and perhaps in a spirit of joyous relief, parents began turning, for the first time, to outside experts for assistance in raising their offspring. Among these was an Italian educator named Maria Montessori, who preached that children must not have lessons drummed into their heads, as in the old school, but must discover them on their own in cheerful environments during early childhood and beyond.

Perhaps the war has made the world a better place. Even the mysterious Chinese Empire is now a republic. The United States immediately recognized the new leaders and moved American troops in to protect our interests. And we have always pursued those interests both over there and over here, for by the time the class of '31 was in grammar school, legislation was passed to make sure the citizens of these new Asian business partners would be permanently prevented from ever coming to this country.

When they were five, the Spanish flu suddenly took over a nation that was on the brink of claiming triumph over tuberculosis. This epidemic added insult to the terrible injury of the war. As five-year-olds they had carved into their memories the tales of someone alarmingly chilled and feverish with the flu—it might have been them—and everyone knew someone who knew someone who had died. Hospitals and doctors could not keep up with the demand for care, as crowds of patients with rasping chests and pale skin took over every ward. Strict quarantines and mild panic spread as quickly as the germs. Local high school gyms were turned into vast wards of agony. Even the cops wore surgical masks in the whipping February wind.

Could you trust anyone with the slightest cough? That was what young class member Richard Nixon, of Whittier, California, must have wondered when his mother took his older brother, Harold, to Arizona so that the dry air might help nurse Harold back to health from TB. At least Harold never caught the flu. It would have been the last of him. Even now, because he remains sickly from his long bout with TB, it is not clear how long he will live.

Aside from disease, the word "trust" has taken on another meaning, an economic one, which kept popping up on the front pages. "Trusts" were everywhere; and for a while, the heroes were the "trustbusters" who were dismantling the monopolistic business empires that controlled the nation. Yet as members of the class have grown older, some of those trust manipulators seemed to be learning better ways to use their ill-gotten gains, as Rockefeller and Carnegie established foundations and Ford improved the pay scale of his assembly line workers. Class members have seen a world evolve from trust titans to trust-busters to trustees, including the now eminently charitable rob-ber barons of their parents' childhoods. During their teens, though, it seemed that the trusts were no longer the most press-ing issue anyhow. Nobody wanted to shake things up too much, as the nation was enjoying its new affluence. Surely, they were told then, you should trust a trust that puts a chicken in every pot. By their late teens, of course, it wasn't a dead chicken they were concerned about. It was a live one, and it was Wall Street, and it had laid an enormous egg. As class members look back, they may well wonder if they were right to trust anything.

* * * *

Wall Street had been rocky a decade before, only then it was not a big egg but a big bomb. Though few of them have ever been directly exposed to terrorism, the stories of anarchists have made them wary. Dynamite has been the weapon of choice for the revolutionaries, and it has been used to raze buildings and bridges and to disrupt all sorts of gatherings. When they were only seven, explosions mangled lower Manhattan at noon, killing and injuring scores of bystanders. The famous statue of George Washington, near the stock exchange, was itself shaken badly (though George is still standing, thank you). A bomb-wielding Hun, who was also a professor, tried to blow up a Senate chamber in Washington, D.C. Presidents along with kings and business leaders were being shot, and while they slumbered tranquilly in their prams, an assassination in Sarajevo in the Balkans set off a massive chain reaction of European states that put out the lights all over Europe for four horrific years. In the United States, private security firms and government agencies have frequently offered stories of great conspiracies for the newspapers, and everyone has followed tales of finding and stopping international criminals like Sacco and Vanzetti. Class members have grown up with an endless back and forth about the guilt or innocence of those two men.

These issues were always worrisome. There were diversions, thank God. The major form of entertainment in their youth centered on the new film palaces that now offered longer movies incorporating sound along with the picture. Those features, along with a weekly serial, *The Perils of Pauline* (who was saved from everything from an ongoing railroad to a mustachioed and heartless landlord), and a Pathé newsreel, offered the perfect way to spend an afternoon or evening. Now with the time saved by the auto and the subways and the typewriter, they had plenty of time to enjoy themselves. By the year they were born, the word "movies" no longer referred to the strange people with megaphones and cameras always "moving" around in order to make these productions. The word now refers to the productions themselves. By the time they were ten, the phrase "I'm going to the movies" was no longer strange. If they lived in big cities, they could enjoy these spectacles in theaters that rivaled the palace of Versailles in their vast spaces, high ceilings with elaborate moldings, and golden and crystalline splendor. They didn't name some of these theaters "The Palace" for nothing.

One of the best examples of the new creative energy of the country was demonstrated by the rise of Hollywood as the capital of this international cinematic enterprise. Charles Pathé had come from France and Charlie Chaplin came from England to be part of this burgeoning industry. Critics have questioned whether film ultimately uplifted and civilized society or corrupted its values. Either way, movies have sounded the death knell of Victorian society, for horses and carriages, strictly controlled images, and outraged innocence have become more passé with every year that goes by. With their roll fights at the Ritz coffee shop, raccoon coats, tomboy looks, and hidden hooch, it seemed that youth, until the Crash, had its own separate culture. The Victorians would never have approved.

Class members can hardly remember the parades, demonstrations, and confrontations—some of them pretty mean—to gain the vote for women. States had begun giving women the vote even before class members were born, and men now seem to have gotten over the fear that women would unethically cancel their husbands' vote with the passage of the Nineteenth Amendment. This generation has grown up around corsetless women who vote for other women, conceal flasks in their garters, bob their hair, engage in public displays of affection, and become telephone operators for the nation or daring ornaments for their husbands. For every innocent flicker sweetheart such as one of the Gish Sisters or Mary Pickford, there seem to be ten flappers named Lulu or Mame.

Freedom has abounded on all fronts. The class of '31 has grown up with self-service markets as an alternative to the familiar friendly neighborhood grocer where only Pat and Mike touched the produce, wrote it up on bags, and brought it to your grandmother's house if the weather was bad. "Classy" new packaging has been attracting consumers' attention in the new stores. Advertisements no longer describe the products calmly and objectively but now offer a touch of poetry and adventure. They appeal to the heart, which has become a loudly ticking organ of mass consumption. It seems there's a Woolworth's, J. C. Penney's, Western Auto, Safeway, or Piggly Wiggly in every town of a certain size.

Camel and Chesterfield cigarettes are among the many new brands available, and even Mother has started smoking. Kraft has always been processing cheese, Hellmann has always mass-produced his Blue Ribbon Mayonnaise, and Welch's grape juice has become the perfect beverage for Sunday dinner, especially since stories circulated of how the secretary of state served it to the British ambassador in Washington. (Besides that, it's also the communion "wine" of choice in the dry South and Midwest.) The downtown residential palaces of industrialists and business leaders have been steadily giving way to retailers and encroaching shopping districts. The friendly pharmacy has become a drugstore where you can buy stuff like Life Savers, the neat new treat in a roll that doesn't melt in the summer as does chocolate.

And with the increased consumption, recyclers and junk men have been expanding their efforts to deal with rubber tires, tin cans, cloth, scrap metal, and cast-iron bathtubs as the new style and opulence replaced them with agitating washing machines and enamel tubs. Invention has always proved itself the mother of necessity—instead of the other way around—as an array of appliances and devices emerged that could find a place in the newly electrical home.

* * * *

In their teens, the class of 1931 experienced the rise of the revolutionary radio, which would encourage this new consumption like never before. For their parents, the radio was the logical next step beyond the wonders of modern telegraphy and the telephone. For class members, however, it has always been the driver of popular culture, the vehicle for spreading new social and artistic movements as well as the variety offered by commercial entertainment. While it may well be another decade before the grand RCA console radio will dominate the parlor (though with the Crash, who knows anymore?), they could always buy or build the simple crystal set that allowed you to pull the signal out of thin air as you hid under the covers at night anywhere in the country and listened to the exciting new "jass" music live on *The Eveready Hour*, coming from WEAF Radio out of New York.

New names have emerged as the royalty of that syncopated beat, those flaring trumpets and boisterous saxophones, those uncanny drums and pianos. Some of them are black folks like Louis Armstrong and Duke Ellington, Fats Waller and Bessie Smith, while others, like Paul Whiteman and George Gershwin, are white. Jazz has its own wild vocabulary, such as "Father Dip," Louis Armstrong's New Orleans nickname, and "that Harlem hotcha," as the jazz club scene in Harlem is called. Hearing this stuff live on radio in places as far away as Kansas and Alabama has always been amazing, but this new cosmopolitan ambiance, with its long tentacles, has also been a paradox, for the very places served by those under-the-covers crystal radios were also influenced by another group—anti-jazz, anti-Negro, anti-Semitic, anti-booze, anti-Darwin and anti-North—with its own preposterous argot, such as "Klavern" and "Kleagle" and "Grand Dragon." Some would say the class of 1931 has reached adulthood in an age of sheeted bigotry. It was in Alabama, back around the time of the Great War, when class member Rosa Louise McCauley (better known as Rosa Parks) began school and noticed that buses took white kids to their schools while Negro children walked to theirs.

Still, it seems everybody has been experimenting with new ideas and new approaches to almost everything, and it is hardly limited to film and radio. Big art exhibitions and concerts in New York City and Chicago have sparked riots and demonstrations claiming that "modern" abstract art is deemed the start of barbarism. Even in football, sportswriters and the Army team were caught completely off guard when Notre Dame advanced the ball using the revolutionary technique of throwing it. There was no rule against it, but nobody had ever thought of it before. Victrolas and Pianolas have brought music into the house and the opportunity to practice all kinds of disturbing new animal dances like the Turkey Trot and the Bunny Hug. Parachute jumping, marathon dancing, and flagpole sitting, municipally supported symphony orchestras in many major cities, and daily reports of new airplane speed and distance records, have kept everyone entertained, wondering what might be next.

Of course not all parents and leaders are sure how much they want to encourage these attitudes and trends. Rumor has it that Woodrow Wilson canceled his second Inaugural Ball out of fear that people might start Ballin' the Jack or dancing the Charleston. The Vatican has officially condemned the tango. Brewers unsuccessfully tried to head off Prohibition by claiming that malt liquor would be a worthy substitute for no booze at all. Class members have always known about Prohibition, but it has been barely enforced and it hasn't affected them as long as Dad could stop off at a "blind pig" in the back of the laundry or hardware store, or at any of thousands of speakeasies, for a refresher. Gin wasn't all that hard to make in an old cast-iron bathtub, and the magazine *Vanity Fair* showed readers how to issue party invitations so that invitees would know there would be booze without the invitation having to say so outright. The decade-long "Noble Experiment" has made folk heroes of Al Capone and Legs Diamond and other mobsters. But maybe if Prohibition ends as Democratic candidate Al Smith urged when they were fifteen, the mobs will go out of business.

Meanwhile, the new urban affluence in many parts of the country has attracted Negroes from the rural South. The migration from the Old South to northern cities and factory jobs has always been changing the tone of the cities, too. The new urban dwellers are bringing with them new artistic forms, as when Harlem's Langston Hughes writes, "I've known rivers ancient as the world and older than the flow of human blood in human veins." But with change comes other blood. Race riots have occurred in East St. Louis and Chicago. Meanwhile, when class members were fourteen, the first movie "talkie" came to the screen, courtesy of Vitaphone, with Al Jolson's black-faced portrayal of a jazz singer who leaves staid family tradition behind to do what he wants in the great metropolis. The addition of sound has impressed young ladies like class member Mary Martin, a talented tomboy from Texas who has grown up imitating the dancing of Ruby Keeler and the singing of Bing Crosby. Unprecedented racial mixing has been reported in city theaters and dance halls. Everybody is humming the "St. Louis Blues."

* * * *

The confidence, affluence, and peace that came after the Great War have prompted the family to invest in a better car rather than a better house. After all, you can't drive downtown in a bathtub, no matter how fancy, plus you could always buy a Ford on the installment plan. Despite the trust issues of their earlier years, confidence was everywhere until their junior year in high school, the year they will always remember as the one that changed their lives. The long lines they were used to as they waited to get into the movie palaces or for a bag of real beef hamburgers at the local White Castle moved overnight to the soup kitchen—and to the banks, as people started pulling out their money. By now it's hard for them to remember when an earlier generation worried that they might become spoiled by zippers!

Faith in the future, which in recent years had never been lacking, has now been lost, and no one knows where to find it. Not only has nearly everyone been affected, sometimes hammered, by the economic collapse, but the decades of immigration have also ended, and more people are now leaving than arriving.

Now, it seems, only Will Rogers is funny. He recently said, "We are the first nation in the history of the world to go to the poorhouse in an automobile." Everyone laughed, but not a great deal.

The
Shadow
Has Always Known

Members of this class were born in 1926 and would have graduated from high school in 1944. If they attended college, they would have graduated in 1948.

Class members include coach Joe Paterno, economist Alan Greenspan, and actress Marilyn Monroe (born Norma Jeane Mortenson, but baptized Norma Jeane Baker).

Harry Houdini, Robert Todd Lincoln, Lizzie Borden, Rudolph Valentino, and the Ford Model T have always been dead.

Mindset List

1. Airline pilots have always flown over the North Pole.

2. Andrew Mellon and Charles Lindbergh have always been going from world-beaters to tragic figures.

3. Radio has always been a handmaiden of commerce.

4. College boys have continued to wear their $39 raccoon coats because after the Crash they could hardly afford a new one.

5. Tents have always been associated with Herbert Hoover and not with the Boy Scouts.

6. They have always used puns in "knock-knock" jokes that make their parents groan.

7. Burma-Shave has always enhanced their road trips with verse.

8. The *Saturday Evening Post* has always been their parents' favorite magazine.

9. Nancy Drew has always driven a roadster and solved the mystery of the hidden staircase.

10. Nearly everyone, it seems, has turned to stamp collecting.

11. Apples have always been associated more with poverty than with sin.

12. They have always called phony things "booshwash."

13. A car in every garage has always expressed, however implausibly, their parents' American Dream.

14. Their mothers have always served themselves by selecting items from the well-stocked shelves of stores called supermarkets, such as those owned and operated by the Great Atlantic and Pacific Tea Company.

15. John Dillinger has always been the man they loved to fear and feared to love.

16. Movies have always talked to them.

17. Babe Ruth, Lou Gehrig, Jimmy Foxx, and Hank Greenberg have always hit incredible numbers of long balls.

18. They grew up learning how to read on Sunday morning with Dagwood's bumbling with Mr. Dithers and Dick Tracy's two-way wrist radios.

19. The Shadow has always known.

20. Radios have always been bigger than most toddlers.

21. They've always laughed when Charlie McCarthy asked W. C. Fields if that's a red traffic light or just his nose.

22. Young men have always grown up wanting to be an all-American boy like Jack Armstrong.

23. Before members of the class started school, hoboes would often come to the back door asking for food in exchange for work.

24. They have grown up waiting each week for packrat Fibber McGee to open the door to his overstuffed closet.

25. The bellboy has always been calling for Philip Morris, and people have always been willing to walk a mile for a Camel.

26. When they were in their cribs, property on Broadway and Wall Street was selling for a record $1,008 per square foot.

27. Henry Ford has offered a forty-hour workweek at five dollars a day—but the company's new "Sociological Department"

has always monitored the men closely so they wouldn't spend the money foolishly.

28. A quarter or less would get them in to see King Kong climb the Empire State Building or watch Jimmy Stewart lecture the U.S. Congress.

29. Bathrooms have always had electrical outlets for razors.

30. Men have always been able to talk openly about B.O., and it's always been okay for them to use deodorant.

31. Men and women have always been able to drink together, and there have always been "powder rooms" for the ladies between rounds of gin.

32. Gas stations have always been designed to look like English cottages.

33. Aimee Semple McPherson, though still saving souls, has always been notorious.

34. The federal government has always licensed pilots and their planes.

35. There have always been sightings of the Lindbergh baby.

36. Gramps and Granny have always preferred to drink Sanka because caffeine made them nervous.

37. Russia has always been a Marxist state.

38. The federal government has always regulated radio frequencies.

39. Long-distance live television has always been possible.

40. The Japanese have never been popular, and the Germans have always been a problem, either because they were too weak or too strong.

41. They've grown up learning the alphabet from FDR.

42. When they were kids, the really smart ones had memorized the names of all five Dionne quintuplets.

43. Thanks to the trench watches used in the Great War, wristwatches have never been considered sissified.

44. They have fond childhood memories of eating "Slo-Baked" Wonder Bread—sliced!

45. Resetting bowling pins, like being a landlord, has always been dangerous.

46. Empty pockets flapping inside out have always been "Hoover Flags."

47. They'll never forget that terrifying moment when the Martians landed in New Jersey.

48. Newspapers have always worried about declining sales due to radio.

49. Badminton and public libraries have always provided inexpensive or free entertainment, especially popular during the Depression.

50. Myrna Loy's dressing gowns as Mrs. Nick Charles were always more luxurious than most evening gowns.

* * * *

In the mid-1930s, photographers, sometimes hired by the Roosevelt administration, recorded the visages of people who were desperate and at times despondent, but determined. The faces of impoverished mothers and their poor children are ever serious, like that of the Tate family in North Carolina some quarter of a century earlier. But while the Tates were serious in order to be respectable, many families in the thirties were serious—their faces lined and drawn and discouraged, their dresses calico *plain—because the Great Depression had ravaged them. Theirs were the images of those driven from the land by the advent of machinery or by the sheer depletion of the soil itself; of those arriving, hope against hope, in new places via their jalopies with fenders held on by twine, living in suburbs of tents. Theirs were the human faces of an economy in which 90 percent of companies cut hours, where only 60 percent of the previously normal work-week was being used, where there was no unemployment insur-ance of any kind, where average American incomes had declined by 40 percent (down to $1,500 a year). Homeless men caught free rides on freight trains, hoping to find work, and flophouses were in such demand that there were not enough beds; gardens were cultivated for survival, and cardboard made do for shoe soles. People couldn't afford to get divorced, but desertion rates shot up. The birth rate was no longer at a replacement level. Several hundred people starved to death, while some families were driven to living in caves or even sewers. Yet the children who grew up in such dire straits lived to see better times and would never again have to endure the squalid conditions cap-tured in these Depression-era photographs. A decade later, the Depression had become history, replaced by a foreign calamity that would finally begin to ease the nation out of the Great Downturn.*

* * * *

Though they will barely remember it, members of the class of 1944 lived through a time both roaring and rich. People had time to bob their hair and sit on flagpoles just for the hell of it. When they were born, the nation seemed happy and well-off.

No one ever said, when class members were toddlers, that maybe the prosperity was false and the wealth unevenly distributed. Nobody important ever said anything about how the too-few real millionaires in the countryside wouldn't be able to sustain all the phony millionaires in the new city skyscrapers. The experts knew as much about what was going on as they did, and they were only two years old.

They've lived through a time of smashed idols. When they were born, Secretary of the Treasury Andrew Mellon was the heroic, pro-business guardian of permanent prosperity. Thin and reserved, with an almost oracular public personality, Mellon advocated lower taxes and government efficiency. He was a highly principled believer in unfettered markets. And it all seemed to work until about 1929. But by the time class members were five, Mellon ranked second only to President Hoover as the national arch-villain. People loved, albeit with bitterness, to show their empty pockets, bereft of cash, as "Hoover flags," and they came to view Mellon as a total incompetent at best and a crook at worst. Heroic in a different way was Charles Lindbergh. When class members were just starting to walk and talk, Lindbergh, boyish and tall, had flown from New York to Paris nonstop and alone. But by the time class members were teens, he was thought to be a Nazi sympathizer. His earlier opposition to American involvement in the war, based on his anti-Jewish and anti-British sentiments, seems to have sentenced him to permanent villainy. Yet it seems to have been only yesterday when Mellon and Lindbergh could do no wrong. They had been America's finest.

Class members have grown up hearing lots of rage about how all the wise men got it wrong. By the time they were in the fourth grade, the question was no longer whether everybody was happy, as the gravelly voiced comic Joe E. Brown might have asked, but whether anybody could spare a dime. Dizzy Dean, a star pitcher for the Gashouse Gang St. Louis Cardinals, always struck a warm chord with them when he said that he developed his pitching arm by killing squirrels in Arkansas so that he'd have something to eat. They've grown up with Franklin Roosevelt's relief programs and alphabet government agencies (WPA, REA, SEC). Old Cal Coolidge, who was president when they were born, wouldn't have liked those programs, but he seems as far removed as Rudolph Valentino.

Coolidge's successor, Mr. Hoover, found his name attached to communities of patched tents known as Hoovervilles, and the apple was associated less with sin and much more with the desperate attempt of the down-and-out to make a few pennies by selling a McIntosh or a Jonathan.

* * * *

Things, they've always been told, weren't always like this. The year before they were born, there was a famous Monkey Trial in Tennessee about whether it was legal to teach that human beings descended from earlier life forms. That stuff has always seemed silly to them—just a relic of the fatuous twenties that must have had time for such absurdity. By the time their older siblings were warning them about how hard first grade was going to be, Pa had lost his job down at the mill or the plant but stayed indoors so that no one would know it. Even if he kept his job, he wasn't sure how much longer he would have it, and he had to take one pay cut after another. They recall how Ma took in washing and started a backyard garden and began doubling the number of tomatoes she canned for the winter. Or she may have gotten a job of her own; Pa didn't like it, but he had no choice. Their older sister might have gotten a cleaning job at the rich lady's house; and if they had a slightly bigger house, their parents might have taken in a boarder or two. When they were toddlers, their family might have bought a brand-new Olds for just $925 (on time, of course) with a sixty horsepower engine, fingertip steering, and easy maneuvering on hills or even in deep mud. Several years later it was a jalopy the family hoped would last long enough to get them to California's sunnier chances, if they had the dough re-mi to get there.

A "loose" girl down the street might have gotten pregnant out of wedlock, and in these times that brought the double trouble of both dishonor and the expense of another mouth to feed. Would she try to do anything about it? But what could she do? A forced marriage due to pregnancy has always been a disgrace, and a back alley "solution" both unspeakable and unspeakably dangerous. Vacations were put off, even part-time household help was dismissed, and nest eggs were always too small, if they existed at all. Going to college was about as likely as turning into Jimmy Cagney or Jean Harlow.

Relatives moved in, despite cramped space, or the family moved in with relatives. They've always had stories about sleeping in the same tiny room with great uncles who snored. When they were little kids playing with old tires, hoboes came to the back door—harmless but hungry and desperate—looking for odd jobs and food. But Ma and Pa did their own hoeing now and had no money to pay anybody anyhow. Women in cities dropped their hemlines and started looking more mature. Times were grim, and the women needed to look the part. The steamy vixens of the previous decade were now out of style.

Though about half the babies were now being born in hospitals, people started wondering whether they could really afford
it. When baby Joe or baby Norma was about to be born, they
remember their parents asking: Wasn't old Aunt Sarah a mid-
wife once? For some folks soup kitchens became the most necessary places in town. Along with church, the "kitchen" became
a place for people to get a bit of free grub and trade rumors
about whether there might be any jobs; and to mingle and share,
in muted tones, hard-luck stories about the humiliation of having to take handouts. Their parents have told them tales about
how the town seemed louder before the Depression. The family
enjoyed a togetherness it never had before. They'd work together
for days to wipe grime off the wall after a "Black Roller" dust
storm. Badminton is a backyard sport requiring little equipment, and it's being played more often than ever before.
Monopoly, with its Pennsylvania Railroad, has always been a
joke in these hard times, but it's a great board game and doesn't
cost much to play; jigsaw puzzles also occupy a lot of time, and
they don't cost anything other than the initial purchase. The
public library has always been the hottest place in town. Phrases
like "down to beans" (a can of the stuff split two or three ways
was often "dinner") and "riding the rails" (it was free, and there
might even be a job along the way) have become new additions
to the American lexicon.

They recall looking down the block and hearing that the
Joneses and the O'Tooles were on relief now, though they didn't
like to talk about it. If they lived in a big city, on summer Sunday afternoons they could walk down the streets and hear a
bellowing priest named Coughlin on the radios wafting his
rants through the open windows. Father Coughlin said he knew
what to do in order to help the Joneses and the O'Tooles

(something about banning all Communists and Jews), but the kids were too young to follow exactly what he meant. Their fathers said that the country might actually go commie before it was all over. They may have had an older sister who dropped from exhaustion in a dance marathon she had entered in order to get a little money and free food; or they may have had an older brother who rode the rails or dug ditches for the Civilian Conservation Corps for nine months in order to make a little money and maybe get an eighth-grade equivalency certificate.

After they finished elementary school, many of them managed to get an after-school job delivering papers, sweeping floors, or bicycling in their tam-o'-shanters to two or three hours of extra labor in a butcher shop or a pencil factory or a bowling alley (where you had to reset pins quickly and flee from the next heavy ball), and things began to get better. Their after-school job in a month or six weeks would pay the five bucks for a needed pair of eyeglasses or buy enough quarts of milk to last their large family for several weeks. Pa at least found government relief work. He might have found work painting the local post office, or if he was another type of painter, he might have put up a new mural there. By then FDR's alphabet agencies had restored some order to the chaos of the Depression, bringing electrical power to areas that had never had it (REA, TVA) and applying scientific knowledge to farming (AAA). Even so, with nearly a fifth of workers still out of work, many in the class of 1944 decided to leave school: even if they couldn't find work, they could at least help with the chores and chop some cotton at home. In Brooklyn young Joe Paterno's parents could barely afford the twenty-dollars-per-year tuition at Brooklyn Prep. He almost had to drop out, but they found the money somehow. Now he's about to enter Brown University, where he'll play football.

* * * *

Times were awful. Times were good. A favorite grandmother might have moved in with them from the next town over and be in the house at close quarters. Mad John Dillinger and Baby Face Nelson made great newspaper copy with their homicidal mayhem and bank thefts. Class members remember their parents saying that everybody was mad at the banks (and at landlords, who were occasionally shot), so it was hard to be mad at Dillinger and Nelson and Pretty Boy Floyd. But their parents asked them not to repeat that at school. Following these thugs was fun, and so was showing off how bright you were by being first in the family to memorize the names of the celebrated Dionne quintuplets of Canada, for Yvonne, Annette, Cécile, Émile, and Marie were the first quintuplets to survive well past infancy.

Dillinger, Nelson, and Floyd would have been nothing without their cars, new or old. Depression or no Depression, the new car models have just kept coming, at least until the war. For the members of this class, cars have never been a rarity in American life, even in the rural sections, where now only about a quarter of the population lives. The Burma-Shave Company has bet largely on the expansion of auto travel, placing their catchy roadside poems (each line painted on a small sign and spaced at intervals of about 200 feet) throughout the nation: Keep well / To the right / Of the oncoming car / Get your close shaves / From the half pound jar / Burma-Shave. When they were born, Henry Ford scrapped the old Model T in favor of the new, modern-looking Model A. Ten years later Chrysler came out with a new Air Flow streamlined car. Somebody must have bought those cars, but most kids could never imagine who could have afforded one.

There's always been a Holland Tunnel and always a need for it. They've grown up reading about roadsters in the Nancy Drew stories. And even now older sisters and brothers have managed to borrow the old family clunker and go off to neck and "spark" in some lovers' lane away from Ma and Pa's prying eyes. It's hard to imagine that the car would ever get more revolutionary than that.

When they were babies, another Babe, Ruth, hit sixty home runs. He has always driven a really fancy car—some say one with sixteen cylinders, though whoever said that might just be blowing smoke. By the time they were out of their cloth diapers, that Babe made more money than President Hoover, and said he deserved it because he'd had a better year than the prez. They've grown up seeing lots of home runs as a norm. Over fifty homers a year seems to them quite possible, even expected. They aren't as astonished by that as are their parents, who grew up with "Home Run" Baker's twenty homers a year. The country's economy may have seemed dead at times, but the ball is no longer dead. Cars don't die as fast either. Even Pa's old used Maxwell runs most of the time.

* * * *

For them, radio has never been a medium for amateurs. It has always been national and commercial, its many frequencies always licensed. As kids they grew up listening to the live broadcasts and laughing during the *Chase and Sanborn Hour* as W. C. Fields threatened to turn Edgar Bergen's dummy, the haughty Charlie McCarthy, into a picket fence. They will never forget that night in October, when they were twelve, as their parents

decided during a commercial break on the Bergen show to listen for a moment to Orson Welles's Mercury Theater. Welles's
dramatization of a Martian invasion was so realistic (complete
with news bulletins) that if you caught the show in mid-broad-
cast you'd have thought it was real; and that is precisely what
Mother and Father and millions of others concluded as they
panicked and repeatedly tried to get a phone call through to the
local police station. They even thought about getting the old
Packard out and fleeing with the entire family—but to where?
This whole episode might turn out to be as close as members of
the class will ever get to the sort of adventure that globe-
trotting Jack Armstrong has on the radio, for Jack, a respected
high school athlete, goes to some new exotic place every week.
Yet he too, an All American boy, has never encountered any
Martians.

FDR has always reassured radio listeners with fireside chats
in that warm Hudson Valley tenor of his. Their grandmothers
tell them that people gather around radios now the way they
used to gather around firesides, and Grandma says she isn't sure
that's a good idea. Whatever happened to the days when people
entertained themselves by talking to one another? But even if
they lived out in the country, the radio has brought them big
bands and jazz. One of their class members, Alan Greenspan
of New York City, once aspired to be a professional clarinetist,
but then he dropped out of the Juilliard School of Music and
headed off to college, hoping to study economics.

On radio the Shadow has always known what evil lurked in
the hearts of men, and they've always marveled at the secret
Lamont Cranston gained in the Far East by which to "cloud
men's minds" and scare the bad guys. It's as though, even in
these economic hard times, at least someone is catching the

cheats, and such standard Shadow foes as the Hand and the Hydra were stand-ins for the rapacious malefactors of great wealth who had caused the Depression. These were the people whose hatred FDR said he welcomed. They might have listened to these shows on the enormous freestanding radio, which was bigger than they were when the family bought it back in far better times.

They could have some fun collecting stamps or lying on the floor on Sunday mornings marveling at Dick Tracy's two-way wrist radio or the bumbling but lovable idiocies of one Dagwood Bumstead. They could giggle while listening in on their older siblings and their use of such words as "booshwash" to mean something was phony or "cheesy" (full of holes). They could join the Jimmie Allen club and learn how to make model airplanes; child stars Mickey Rooney and Shirley Temple were both proud members. They could read *Boys' Life* and learn how to be dependable and brave, or *American Girl* and learn how to be decent and demure. As they got older, the boys might have turned to other fare, such as a "Tijuana Bible," those notoriously secret comic strips that featured rather scandalous sexual behavior. On a more innocent note they could tell "knock-knock" jokes and make their parents flinch at the horror of the puns (Knock-knock. Who's there? Will. Will who? Will you go away so I won't have to tell you any more of these corny jokes?).

* * * *

The greatest delight has always been found at the movies. They've always been able to get into a picture show for about two or three dimes. Since they were three, they could go to a moving picture that talked. Talkies have ruined the careers of actors like the squeaky-voiced John Gilbert, but they've always adored Bette Davis for her wicked cunning and Joan Crawford for her resolute bravery in the face of woe. Clark Gable, devil-may-care but always handsome and trustworthy, watched in shock as Claudette Colbert lifted her skirt in order to hitch a ride, and they will always recall snickering in shock right along with him when they were just eight years old.

Of course there have always been limits. Their parents were reluctant to let them watch Bela Lugosi's Dracula suck some blood. Grandma has always said there was something smutty about all that, but they remember sneaking in anyhow. Their parents and grandparents have always been pretty straitlaced. Even out in the home of the heavenly movies, Los Angeles, Norma Jeane Baker's mother may have married a man named Mortenson (even though he was not Norma Jeane's biological father) in order to escape the stigma of being an illegitimate mother. At last report Norma Jeane was going to try for a modeling career. Like her classmates, she has always loved the picture shows, and just a few years after graduation they might recognize her on-screen, but with a new name—Marilyn Monroe. As she's grown up, she has imagined that Clark Gable is her father. She was a big fan of the late Jean Harlow, with her blond hair the same platinum shade as the lining in the box that their mother placed her wedding ring in, if she hasn't already pawned it at the local pawnbroker's shop in order to put food on the table. A really valuable fifty-dollar ring, offered as security for a loan at 3 percent interest, would go far until the family could get back on its feet. It would buy lots of gallons of gasoline at ten cents a gallon (now available at those new gas stations designed to look like English cottages), plus many loaves of bread at five cents per loaf, and perhaps even a new winter coat for sixteen dollars or less. And if the family situation doesn't improve, well, Mom never *really* needed that ring anyhow. Did she?

The movies with their black and white images were projected onto a highly reflective surface with high silver content, which has always been referred to as the silver screen. Even if class members lived in a small town, the silver screen brought them lithe and lilting dancing girls kicking their heels around fountains; stories of cruel but somehow sympathetic gangsters; and (when they were thirteen) an Atlanta burning during the Civil War and rascally but glamorous southerners like Gable who dared to say "damn" on the screen. They themselves have never been allowed to utter that word at home.

They have always had vivid memories of how the silver screen helped them feel better about the Depression—either by insulting it or by celebrating its upside. Walt Disney's Mickey Mouse has always been a solid middle-class citizen; Mickey has never been the brat their parents recall. The Three Little Pigs have always sung "Who's Afraid of the Big Bad Wolf?" in defiance of the economic wolf at the door of millions. They saw these Disney movies with their parents, and though they were only seven or eight at the time, they saw lots of grown-up movies with their parents, too. They cheered and laughed with their parents as films poked fun at the Depression and at the tuxedoed stuffed shirts who must have started the whole "damned thing" (as Rhett Butler might have put it).

Groucho Marx has always teased mercilessly that rich old dowager played by Margaret Dumont. "Your hair, your lips, your eyes: everything about you reminds me of you—except you." Nick Charles, the "Thin Man," played by William Powell, was an aristocratic drinking detective, but he has always known every cardsharp and pickpocket in town, as if the Depression has made everybody more equal to one another. With the Thin Man they were always able to get all the glamour of raffish café society and a taste of democracy at the same time. In other films Henry Fonda's cap and dirty overalls offered a stark contrast to Fred Astaire's top hat and tails, but moviegoers enjoyed both men's on-screen portrayals. Indeed, the Hollywood of their day has always offered them a look at just about everything, from poverty with little mercy to luxury with little guilt.

* * * *

As they've grown closer to adulthood, they were always a bit too young to enlist in the military, which was fully engaged on two fronts during World War II. Now that there are signs that Hitler is crumbling, they *are* getting in but have reason to hope that the thing will be over soon, at least in Europe. All the boys in the class expect to be sent to Japan, though, for a long war. There's December 7, 1941, and the USS *Arizona* in its watery grave to be avenged.

Meanwhile, since the White House announced the Japanese attack on Pearl Harbor that cold Sunday afternoon in December three years ago, they and their families have been caught up in the war, which has replaced the Depression as the number one topic. Lots of them have sisters who were involved with some older feller. He may have been lost in North Africa; no one quite knows how. The last thing you want to see is somebody from Western Union showing up with a telegram, accompanied by your local pastor. The movies themselves have taken up the theme of suffering for the good of others. Humphrey Bogart in *The Maltese Falcon* has forsaken a lovely woman because he thought avenging his partner's murder took priority, and in *Casablanca* he gave up Ingrid Bergman herself because fighting Nazis came first. About four years earlier, when they were fourteen, President Roosevelt declared that this generation, including the teenagers in the class of 1944, had a date—not with Greta Garbo or Clark Gable, but with destiny.

Their family has continued to drive its car a long time, even though it is getting old. Steel and rubber have been rationed for only three years, but it seems like forever. Everyone has been wondering for some time whether there will ever be new cars and tires again. No one has forgotten what they were doing that December afternoon. Most of them had just gotten home from church and were sitting down to the best meal (with meat!) of the week. Some of them were listening to the New York Giants football game when the broadcast was interrupted by a monotone news bulletin that all of a sudden made the game seem trivial.

Since then, women, because hosiery was often not available, used eye makeup to draw seams on the backs of their bare legs in order to simulate the real thing. They would apply some sort of thick foundation liquid, walk around in their undies until it dried, and then apply the mascara, only to find that it smeared as soon as they sat down. About two years ago Mom noticed that the government was building Quonset huts for the military over on the local college campus. In high school the students have had to learn the locations of faraway places like Midway and Okinawa. Stars like Bob Hope and Ronald Reagan have sold war bonds. Companies have proudly advertised their products as also helping in the war effort. Navy men spiff up their hair with Vitalis or Brylcreem, and the makers of the products let you know it. Every little bit, even good hair cream, helps win the war. The war has been hard, and when they were in their midteens the news was almost always bad. But now that they're about to graduate from high school (some of them, anyhow), the bad times seem to have had an energizing effect, as though that woman named Rosie, featured in all the war ads, has always been a happy riveter.

* * * *

They've always sensed that on the other side of the war there'll be more than just the bluebirds of peace and happiness over the white cliffs of Dover. But they have no idea what that something else will be. They're pretty sure, though, that it won't be war with our great ally Russia. And the boys expect that the Rosies of this world will be heading back to the kitchen soon and planning to stay there for a while. FDR will still be president when they first get to vote in 1948, just one year past their twenty-first birthday. Many of them plan to vote for him. Who knows? Hell, maybe by then the war will be over.

Fluoride
Has Always Been Controversial

Members of this class were born in 1939 and graduated from high school in 1957. If they went to college (increasingly likely after World War II), they would have graduated in 1961.

Members of the class include singer Marvin Gaye, alleged assassin Lee Harvey Oswald, and baseball player Carl Yastrzemski.

Nobel Prize–winning poet William Butler Yeats, famous writer of Westerns Zane Grey, actor Douglas Fairbanks Sr., and Sigmund Freud have always been dead.

Mindset List

1. They've never seen a business cycle allowed to run its course without the government's taking into account its impact on human lives.

2. "Water closets" have always been called "bathrooms."

3. As they slept peacefully in their cribs, most members of their parents' generation were strongly opposed to any U.S. intervention in foreign conflicts.

4. Before some of them could walk, their fathers registered for the draft.

5. Thanks to radio, their parents have always been able to hear the sounds of war in their living rooms.

6. Thousands of them can barely remember their late fathers.

7. They've grown up with great American acronyms, such as KP, SNAFU, MAD, and UNIVAC.

8. "Zoot suits" have always been notorious.

9. Their first *Time* Man of the Year was Adolf Hitler.

10. Their uncles might have received letters addressed "Dear John" while serving overseas.

11. They've never known an America of persistent high unemployment or of low defense budgets.

12. Their parents have always lamented the government's withholding taxes from their paychecks.

13. When they started school, they already knew how to pronounce "Okinawa," "Iwo Jima," "kamikaze," and "Nagasaki."

14. As they've grown up, social commentators have always worried about their timidity.

15. They've always been able to get Social Security benefits from a deceased parent.

16. Their parents, sitting in the "dens" of their "ranches," have often said they would never vote for a divorced man.

17. Their being called a "JD"—or accused of smoking "Mary Jane"—has always been a disgrace for their folks.

18. "Do-it-yourself" and "togetherness" are popular terms that have defined life in their suburban homes.

19. They've seen overalls and uniforms being replaced by flannel suits, both blue and gray.

20. Their parents firmly believe that orthodontics is necessary.

21. Women who were once jeep makers are now homemakers.

22. They haven't used a bottle of ink since seventh grade, and for a lark they test their Paper Mate ballpoints to see if they really will write through butter.

23. As they've become teenagers, two southern Kings—in civil rights and rock 'n' roll—have been stirring up trouble.

24. Chips and dip in their special dish on TV trays have replaced popcorn in paper sacks on Saturday night.

25. They would note the location of the official Civil Defense (CD) fallout shelter on their way to school, and once they got there, they were drilled to "duck and cover."

26. Europe has always been a battleground or a chessboard.

27. When they were tots, "Super" referred to a man; now that they are teens, it refers to a bomb.

28. They might have heard grown-ups muse about the wisdom of unleashing Chiang, thinking that was an odd name for a dog.

29. Subversives could be anywhere.

30. Water fluoridation is now a toothy issue.

31. Their first toys were "Little Army Nurse" and "Blackout Kit."

32. Betty Grable accompanied their fathers to war in order to remind them of what they were fighting for.

33. The Tuskegee Airmen have always been fighting one war or another.

34. They might recall seeing a doubleheader during the war, between the Rockford Peaches and the Kalamazoo Lassies.

35. Some of them have gotten more in a weekly allowance than a whole family earned in a week during the Depression.

36. Before doing their homework after school, they were amused by their younger siblings as they laughed with Clarabell, Chief Thunderthud, Dilly Dally, Flub-a-dub, and Princess Summerfall Winterspring.

37. As teens they've worn Polaroids to the beach *and* to the movies.

38. Since it will cost them about two thousand dollars in tuition over four years, their parents have always been saving to send them to college.

39. They've always tried to avoid their mothers' Tupperware parties.

40. They've left *Your Hit Parade* for Alan Freed, Andy Hardy for Jim Stark, and the doggie in the window for a screamin' hound dog.

41. They've enjoyed watching their younger siblings wear coonskin hats and make things with Play-Doh.

42. They don't dig being square, and have often gone steady despite Mom's suggestion that they play the field.

43. For their fathers, briefcases have become almost as essential as socks.

44. To college they'll take their Wham-O Flying Saucer (better known as a Frisbee), a curvy plastic chair, a portable typewriter, and a pole lamp.

45. Their parents read a book by Dr. Spock in the morning before the kids woke up and a book by Dr. Kinsey in the evening after the kids went to sleep.

46. "Teenager" has always designated a separate state of mind.

47. In high school they've made the drag in their own hot rods, raked and decked complete with duals, and maybe even white skins.

48. "Expecting" is okay; "pregnant" is not.

49. If they've been troublesome teens, their moms might have gone to Miltown.

50. Since they were teens, radio has always been fading into the background.

* * * *

In 1950 an enterprising photographer named Alfred Eisenstadt took a shot of a high-strutting drum major at the University of Michigan. He was practicing his step for some big football game—probably the bitterly fought annual contest with Ohio State. Behind him are several kids aged from about seven to maybe eleven. One of them might have been a member of the high school class of 1957, and several of them could have been a little brother or sister. Oblivious to the terrible worries of their parents about Communism in China, Korea, and Russia or at home, they are obviously enjoying this bit of high jinks. They seem carefree and well nourished. Though the drum major is obviously no Nazi, it's as though these kids know that their parents helped win the war over Hitler, so now they are free to mock any semblance of goose-stepping. In some ways this is a scene of America triumphant. These were the kids in the land that won the war and emerged as the most victorious and influential nation on the planet by far. In this photo they are in the country that used the war to beat the Depression. Unlike their often grim-looking older cousins in their tam-o'-shanters or overalls, hoping to rake up a spare dime or two collecting junk or hauling hay or anything else they could do in order to help their struggling families, these kids all look as though they're already getting allowances. It also seems as though they are starting to develop a little fun-loving skepticism of conventional authority. This striking image of cheerful and innocent strutting is an apt preview of the high school class of 1957 (college class of 1961), as they are beginning to lift off, like the United States' burgeoning missile program, into eventual adulthood.

* * * *

When members of this class were born in 1939, the United States was warily at peace. If they had been born in early

September 1939, news of their arrival might have had competition, as Americans listened to the radio nearly all day to hear
the British declaration of war on Germany announced as it
happened. As these infants slept peacefully in their cribs, the
great majority of Americans wanted the United States to stay
the hell out of this thing. As members of the class began to walk
and talk, and as their parents began to long for the day when
they would finally graduate from their cloth diapers, the nation
was in constant debate about the advisability of siding with
England over Germany and about resisting Japanese expansion
in the Pacific. It was a jittery time, but the kids, once again, slept
right through it. They would have had no distinct memory of
December 7, 1941, when all debate ended. If they had an uncle
and aunt who received a knock on the door from a minister and
a man in uniform, bearing an unbearable telegram from the
War Department about a son lost in Hawaii, it was a grim family story they would hear about later.

Even before Pearl Harbor, while their mothers were putting
talcum powder on their bottoms to prevent rash, their fathers
had signed up for the draft, hoping they would never have to go
anywhere near conflict. As class members have grown up, many
have done so in the absence of fathers who never came back
from the war and whom they can't recall beyond family photos.
Now many of them have stepfathers who were luckier. Their
mothers may have gone to work in order to help the war effort.
If "Rosie the Riveter" had been their mom, her muscular arms
would have no difficulty picking them up. But Rosie may well
have had trouble taking care of them during long work hours.
Agnes Meyer, whose husband, Eugene, published the *Washington Post*, remembers stories of kids left by themselves in locked
cars or movie houses.

So sometimes there was no place for little Junior or Sis other than at the movie theater watching endless reshowings of *Lassie Come Home* until Mom got off her shift. The parents of the class of '57 had expected something different. Dad would go to work, while Mom would stay home or maybe work as a secretary, a salesgirl, a clerk, a typist, or a practical nurse. Their parents had expected to have to struggle against the ongoing impact of the Big Crash. Then suddenly Dad was bombing Dresden while Mom was making jeeps.

As the class of 1957 were slowly emerging from cribs, there was only one real subject in the land to which they were born: the War. Ads were "double-barreled": if you advertised toothpaste or cigarettes, by government decree you had to say how they were helping win the war. Hollywood films were less about individual heroism and more about the group's sticking together. Their moms might have gone through several hankies watching "weepies" (such as *Since You Went Away*) about the subject of men having to leave the family behind and go to war. But with the coming of war came travel their fathers could never have dreamt of just a few years before; so KILROY WAS HERE graffiti, a sign of American presence, was found, it seemed, in nearly every bathroom stall from Tunisia to Turin.

For everyone back home, war meant meatless Tuesdays and Fridays or cutting the meat off the lamb chop for the kids while Mom chewed on what was left—unless she had a new recipe for Spam, which she might serve along with Uncle Ben's new "converted" rice. The kids did their part by tagging along with older brothers and sisters in the Scouts or Campfire Girls as they collected scraps and newspapers, or they helped Mom plant and keep up the victory garden. There were always stories about unpatriotic people down the street who didn't do their part because they kept their iron fence and gate around the house and wouldn't turn it in for the war effort, as real Americans did. Their elders wore Windsor-knot ties or blue uniform dresses with military-style jewelry. Smart-aleck older siblings, inspired by *Duffy's Tavern*, a popular radio program that offered a break from news of the war, answered the phone with "Where the elite meet to eat—Duffy speaking," while older folks took Serutan ("natures" spelled backward) to keep them regular on the home front.

As they have grown beyond diapers and their toddler years, they have learned to pronounce "Okinawa" and "Nagasaki." They have wondered where the big "bulge" was in the Battle of the Bulge. They were thrilled when a letter from Dad came from overseas, in which he always told them how much he missed them and how he had made all sorts of promises to himself to do better in life if he survived and how they were not to worry. If they grew up in the Midwest, they might recall rooting for Rockford or Milwaukee in one of the women's professional baseball games popular during the war, when the men were elsewhere, thinking about things other than balls and strikes. They began first grade at the time the war ended. They will never forget the crowds and the hoopla and the ticker tape and then the endless *red* tape relating to when Dad was getting home at last or, much worse, the endless red tape surrounding what may have happened to him.

After his return home, Dad might have become a member of the government's 52/20 club: twenty bucks a week for fifty-two weeks in order to help him get resettled in civilian life. They remember how tough things were for a while as Mom, used to running the show, had to yield to Dad's authority once again about purchases and bills; and how Dad, now remembering those vows he'd made in the war, had to think about whether he wanted to try something big, like going to college or buying a house or starting a business. Dad has always been reticent about the war and has said flatly that he doesn't want to talk about it. It's clear, though, that he has seen things, and done things.

So have they, in a way. Their elders may have clung to the radio to get reports from Ed Murrow and his boys, but the members of this class have climbed over rocks in parks and vacant lots to create their own versions of machine-gun nests as they fired on imaginary Japs and Germans, whom they'd learned about through film and TV. They've also left KILROY WAS HERE on places that they shouldn't have. They would have to wait until the television documentary *Victory at Sea* was broadcast in their teens in order to learn more than their uncles would share about naval battles.

Now Dad's been home for over a decade. Everything is quite respectable, and if Dad has killed people or ever taken sulfa for a "social disease," along with taking that photo of Betty Grable with him in his helmet—well, it doesn't bear thinking or talking about. It has always been past time for everything to become normal again. Mom might well have continued working outside the home, but it was more likely that she became a "homemaker," even if she had once wielded a wrench or shot a rivet gun.

Mom isn't the only one who's had to adjust to civilian life. So have Negro servicemen, and no postwar adaptation has been more dramatic than that of the Tuskegee Airmen. Class members may have grown up hearing about these guys—though they won't remember the War Bond posters that featured them. They trained for combat service in Alabama in the summer of 1941 and later performed admirably in bombing the Germans from the air while, on the ground, they endured Army facilities and services both segregated and inferior. Now that the Airmen are back home, the crimson Red Tail insignia on their warplanes left far behind, they are working through civilian life again in conditions that remain separate and unequal; some of them have gotten jobs as air instructors at flight schools, but mainly those owned by other Negroes. Class members, if they knew about this saga or thought about it, might well sense that the Airmen haven't gotten a fair deal, but this sort of thing is not on a top rung of class members' ladder of values and most likely never will be.

Everything seemed to brighten with the families reunited (though people were already fearing a "cold war" with Communists). As kids they were reminded nightly of how lucky they were because children were starving in Europe (later it would be China), and they'd better clean their plates. CARE packages soon became a popular way for Americans to show that they cared for less fortunate people who were facing serious difficulty, whether war, accident, or natural disaster. Radio, meanwhile, once the source for news of European havoc, now began to offer entertaining distractions as listeners competed with the *Quiz Kids* or learned what happened to people who didn't tell the truth and had to take the consequences. When they came home at noon from second- and third-grade classes, they grabbed a Campbell's soup and sandwich lunch with Mom with fifteen-minute episodes of *Helen Trent* and *The Second Mrs. Burton* on the radio as a backdrop before heading back. Class members focused on the man who could leap tall buildings in a single bound, and they perfected the art while jumping off their beds in a red cape. Every one of them knew the "William Tell Overture," though they didn't know it was called that. Some wore black masks. All of them could sing "You Are My Sun-shine." By the time they were about ten, television was widely available, but no one would watch it too much at first because rumor was it wasn't good for your eyes, especially if you watched it in a dark room.

When they were still in grammar school, inflation might have become a problem, with all that government wartime spending. But members of the class of 1957 have never known a time when it wasn't the government's obligation to fix the economy. The Soviet Union has become our foe—that didn't take long—and Europe, once a war zone, has now become a chessboard of political struggle. Germany has always been a different sort of problem—not too strong this time, but too weak. China, once our favorite nation, has gone Commie. The Japanese, once our great foe, have now become friendly and cooperative. The Soviets have the atomic bomb, and no one knows just how mad the now-dead Stalin might have been. The war in Korea has been called a "police action," but it's unlike any police action their parents have ever seen before, and Dad may have had to go away and fight again, this time in frigid circum-stances against a formidable Asian land foe. When that conflict was over, they wondered why there were no ticker-tape parades like the ones they saw when they were six.

While Johnny and Judy of the class of '57 were unleashing their dog in the local park, their parents talked of "unleashing Chiang" to invade the Red Chinese mainland. Understandably puzzled, their twelve-year-old minds didn't know any dogs named Chiang. Their parents believed that fluoride from Procter & Gamble would prevent tooth decay, but one of their neigh-bors has said that with all the spies around nowadays, no one can say for sure that putting the stuff in the drinking water isn't subversive, brought to us by the same traitors that lost China and gave the Soviets the bomb. Some folks agree with him, but more important is what their *parents* agree on: that even slightly crooked teeth may well need braces.

* * * *

The government has practically paid Dad's way through college and helped him buy their new home. America has always seemed rich and getting richer. It never suffered any damage whatever on its mainland from the war. If Europe has been overrun with desperate refugees, if Japan is still searching through radiated rubble, and if the Soviets have lost a million people in just six years, the United States is as victorious as the high school football team the year they won state. Their parents never expected to be so well-fixed. They never dreamed of brand-new ranch homes with enormous picture windows, a gleaming white refrigerator, and neat if small lawns and barbecue pits in back; of phonographs that would change hi-fi records automatically; or of seventeen-inch TV screens on which they could watch old movies they thought they'd never see again.

Their parents never thought that "live" would refer not to being alive but to a TV show's being presented in real time, as they were watching. They never thought a "development" would be where they would be living. They never expected to watch moving pictures while eating from TV trays in their own home, rather than with popcorn bags in their laps at the local theater. They never imagined that big movie epics, such as big-budget religious films, would get them to break faith with Lawrence Welk on Saturday nights. They never thought they'd be able to buy a swept-wing new car that looked as if it could fly, or at least a "late-model" used one. And they never dreamed that with the new "wonder drugs" you could actually send the kids to school if they had sniffles instead of requiring them to stay home in bed—and that Dad's insurance, offered by his employer, would pay for it.

Members of the class of 1957 began to get weekly allowances in excess of what whole families made two decades earlier, to spend on Clearasil, Cokes, movie mags, *Seventeen*, and (less often) savings bonds for college. They would run around in horizontally striped T-shirts and cuffed jeans, driving their mothers crazy by yelling "Say the secret word" or "Just the facts, ma'am" over and over again—until Mom kicked them out of the house and turned to *The Guiding Light* on TV for diversion. Miltown tablets have become proven tranquilizers of tension. Rumors have circulated in the suburbs that some of the moms really had something more than water in that spray bottle on the ironing board. The family has learned the difference in TV reception between VHF and UHF and has struggled with the "rotator" on the TV set that adjusts the silvery antenna that has always sprouted from the roof. Dad, by now having finished his degree in accounting, marketing, or management, has always driven to work (though the new roads all seem to lead *out* of town rather than into it), and he has always felt naked without his briefcase—though of late he has made the radical move of occasionally going hatless. Grandfather, meanwhile, is near retirement but wears a suit only on Sundays or for weddings and funerals. He farms or is a lineman for the county or owns his own filling station. But more and more younger men are wearing suits every day now—a sign of the new professionalism and prosperity.

Not everyone has always been so lucky. One member of their class, a young Negro named Marvin Gaye, has grown up in the Washington, D.C., housing projects listening to something called doo-wop and being beaten by his preacher father on a regular basis. Another class member, Lee Oswald, has been in twenty-two different schools, was raised by an unstable mother, and has joined the marines, where he would be taunted as "Ozzie Rabbit" and describe himself as a socialist.

But for many members of the class of 1957, an unprecedented cornucopia of consumption and convenience now pervaded the land. 78 rpm records, quite breakable and lasting only three minutes or so, have now been replaced by "unbreakable" 33s, those LPs that go on seven times as long before needing a change. Even better, many families displayed handsome walnut cabinets containing a full entertainment system (TV, radio, and record player that held as many as five long-playing records at a time, changing them automatically). Class members themselves love 45 rpms, small and easy to carry around, and capable of endless stacking on a stout plastic converter that's standard equipment on portable record players. In every town of any size at all is a record store complete with soundproof listening booths. If the Colt .45 conquered the West, another 45 conquered the class of 1957—now all the Wurlitzer jukeboxes play these little records with one song on each side.

And with each new product and each new trend has come something more important: even more so than their predecessors in the 1920s, members of the class of '57 have made the entire nation conscious of them as a tribe apart. They are on their way to becoming a separate culture, complete with that blend of jazz, blues, and hillbilly now known as "rock 'n' roll."

If anyone realizes that in Negro musical circles the term refers to sex, no one is admitting it. Had their parents given them ballroom dance lessons, they were wasted, for with the "back-beat" of rock 'n' roll, no one needs instruction in order to dance—one needs only to be young, hormonal, and mobile. When they were thirteen, "Tennessee Waltz" was the top song in the land. Now that they are about to graduate from high school, two-thirds of the top sixty songs are rock 'n' roll, with their suggestive "leer-ics," as one scoffing but witty adult has put it. Ever since they were in junior high, it's been a trip—from Alan Freed, the Cleveland deejay who first dared to spin "rhythm and blues," to Johnny Ray, the Nabob of Sob who wept his songs on the floor, to Bill Haley and the Comets rocking 'round the clock like a second hand on uppers. Soon enough has come the freedom of wheels, of the car radio and the portable record player you could buy on time with your allowance for only about forty-eight bucks or the transistor radio you could get for twenty-five. They could escape from Mom and Dad, listen to music in their own rooms, bop in the drive-in parking lot while waiting for a thirty-five-cent milk-shake, tune in to deejays who took voice lessons from Negroes in order to sound gravelly and black, and thrill to Buddy Holly's falsetto hiccup.

It's been an idyllic time of saddle shoes, dress hems about fourteen inches from the ground, going steady as symbolized by "broken heart" bracelets (that way you don't have to worry about making conversation with every new boy or girl around), Bunny Hops, pep clubs, pimple anxieties, hair tonic that makes the flat-top bristles stand up straight and strong, and, once Elvis got going, "Hound Dog Orange" or "Cruel Red" lipstick. And always in the background, whether at proms or sock hops or pajama parties, has been the beat of Chuck Berry or Little Richard or Fabian or the Everlys. Many mayors and preachers and parents are outraged by such barbarity, but the kids, still obsessed with getting four athletic letters in high school or getting a Mixmaster or an Osterizer at their engagement showers, consider these pleasures harmless enough. Flush with the new prosperity, members of the class have been marrying earlier than the previous generation did, so a good percentage of this high school class will be hearing wedding bells soon. A poll has revealed that among the girls' ideal husbands are Tony Curtis and President Eisenhower.

In the meantime, though, there is always home: a realm of multiple phone jacks, drip-dry pants, refrigerators with Lazy Susan rotating trays, Formica countertops (which some say resemble Jackson Pollock's drip-drop paintings), elegantly understated Danish Modern furniture, flip-top cartons of filtered cigarettes (no cancer!), chaise lounges, infinite amounts of chrome, many-colored washers and dryers, and Crest toothpaste now with Fluoristan ("Look, Mom! No cavities!"). Mom and Dad sleep in the same bed, but no one on TV does. Mom can beautify her hair by applying Miss Clairol's colors, though only her hairdresser knows for sure. Foodarama (double-door) fridges contain bountiful supplies of Cheez Whiz and TV dinners. By using Dial with hexachlorophene, anyone in the family can get as dirty as they want without worrying about germs.

* * * *

When they were born, their older siblings tell them, the family always ate together. Now that they are about to graduate from high school, it often does so in shifts, as Dad may be working late at the office or Mom may have a book or canasta club to go to. Family members sometimes have to take turns watching their favorite TV shows and thus have their Swanson's frozen dinners at different times. Or maybe Mom would just rather throw a few of these TV dinners into the Hotpoint oven and spend the evening working on her painting by numbers or learning how to play the ukulele. Even so, the family tries to spend a lot of time together. Thus do-it-yourself often means do-it-as-a-family, whether that involves putting together the new bookshelves or repainting the living room walls with quick-dry latex paint. Scrabble is huge now, and Dad and Junior have always enjoyed putting together model airplanes, or playing baseball together, as class member Carl Yastrzemski has always done with his dad out by their Long Island potato farm. For their younger siblings there has been the zaniness of Silly Putty and Mr. Potato Head. They've also spent long hours just sitting in the den and paging through that fascinating book *The Family of Man*, with moving photographs of family events—from births to deaths and everything in between—enjoyed by people all over the world.

Although their grandparents may once have bought them a springy Slinky for their birthdays, they may well have no stairs for it to slither down, for many ranch houses during the period were built on a single slab, with no basements, enormous picture windows, privacy guaranteed by the living room's facing the backyard, built-in television sets, two or three bedrooms, and maybe a family room or "den." The den has become the center of family life, while the "living room" is a sort of museum piece, set aside for more formal entertainment. These rooms are cooled by individual unit air conditioners, but before that they had noisy fans, installed in small and hard-to-reach attics, that sucked hot air out. The family takes a week's vacation every year, nearly always in cars that have gotten bigger and longer and more and more like jet airplanes, with their elaborate fins. Every year the dashboard looks more like that of a cockpit.

Yellowstone or Acadia or the Smokies or the Cascades have always been popular destinations—and after they were fifteen, there was Disneyland in California. On the way they could always stay in one of the thousands of new "motels" and stop at hamburger shops that might sport a neon rocket as a distinctive road sign. Back home, Dad wouldn't be caught dead in the kitchen, but he is happy to preside over the barbecue kettle in the backyard on summer afternoons, perhaps wearing a YOU'RE THE GREATEST chef's apron. Otherwise the kitchen is Mom's domain. She goes to the beauty parlor, but Dad is the "beautician" of the lawn. They have, both of them, always sipped martinis and struck it Lucky with cigarettes. After all, they helped win the Second World War.

* * * *

Because class members are only about eighteen now, they have scant awareness that intellectuals see them and their older siblings as silent and timid. One professor, named Leslie Fiedler, says that this generation should be mocking their elders, but they seem instead to be almost too nice. A survey reveals that college students don't want to become personnel managers when they graduate because then they might have to fire someone. Their parents say that they will never vote for someone like

Adlai Stevenson because he's an egghead (he's also divorced), and class members have sometimes wondered if this refers to Stevenson's being bald. They're confused because their parents like Ike, yet Ike is bald, too.

But they've always sensed that the grandfatherly Ike is what their parents want: not a lot of change in any direction; keep the New Deal but give it a rest. Still, not all seems as stable and predictable as the next sock hop in the school gym. There's that Negro woman down in Alabama who wouldn't give up her seat on the bus, and those Negro students in Arkansas who required the protection of the U.S. military as they entered high school. And there's always been that radical Supreme Court. On the other hand, Negro members of the class might well take a different view and regard these developments as auguring hope for improved lives in the 1960s or '70s.

They've never had to work in order to support their families, but they do work after school, as baggers in grocery stores or as carhops at the drive-in or as soda jerks in drugstores. Once upon a time those positions would have been seen as jobs that grown men needed, but no longer in this wealthy nation. Almost everything is portable now, from typewriters to record players to radios. They can go to the beach and listen to rock music while frolicking in the sand. Once, when they were much younger, they *listened* to the radio, along with their parents, and heard *The Lone Ranger* and *Mr. Keene, Tracer of Lost Persons*. Now they *watch* TV, while the radio, which has gone local, has become more like the sky or the scenery or the easy chair— something pleasant in the background, unless they are dancing to "Blue Suede Shoes" or "Blueberry Hill." Just a few years back, it seems, they were watching Snooky Lanson sing "O! My Papa!" on *Your Hit Parade*. The family no longer sits around and listens to the radio, as earlier families had sat around the fire-place; now you catch the news on the radio or mention some-thing you heard on the radio. But only your grandmother ever *listens* to it any more.

When their parents were about their age, they enjoyed the reassuring life lessons learned by earnest Andy Hardy. Now their parents' children can't quite help but be drawn to a primi-tive and mumbling cyclist like Marlon Brando, or to a troubled but appealing rebel like James Dean. In a trend that their grand-parents and even their parents could have hardly envisioned, the members of the class of '57 expect to go to college in a land that now confers nearly eight hundred thousand bachelor's degrees *a year*. Carefree and anything but square, they dig heading off to school with their portable Smith-Coronas, their pole lamps, their Wham-O platters, and their groovy plastic desk chairs.

The whole country is having a fit about JDs (juvenile delin-quents), and Estes Kefauver, a prominent senator who has cam-paigned in a Davy Crockett coonskin hat, claims they are a national disgrace. Most of these kids are not in that category, even if some of their chums do have modest ducktail haircuts and drive old jalopies now turned into hot rods with dual tail-pipes and bull-nosed hoods with the ornaments removed and maybe even whitewall skins for tires. Tonight they'll all make the drag again, maybe on a road near one of those new interstate highways they're breaking sod for everywhere. A few of their buddies might even wear a leather jacket with "Stagger Lee" painted across it. But it doesn't mean anything. It's not like he's smoking Mary Jane.

* * * *

They've heard about a group of crazies, mostly in big cities, who are called "Beats." Complete with turtlenecks, dark glasses, berets, beards, and bongo drums in coffee houses, they talk about "cats" and "bread" and "having a gas" and claim to be "beaten down" by society. Maybe they're called "beats" because of the beating of the bongos. But these kids aren't beats. They're nice kids. They make money, not bread, and call females girls, not chicks. "Crazy," to them, means insane, not "far out."

Of course the beatniks have never been the only weird things around. Ever since class members were three-year-olds, zoot suits were the suspect garb of mindless rebellion. Those bright jackets as thick as Mom's drapes, with wide lapels and high pleated trousers pegged closely at the ankles, were first worn by black jazz men in Harlem; but most notoriously they were the uniform of draft-dodging Latino gangs during the middle of the war. Ever since then the zoot suit has become the unmistakable symbol of everything disrespectable.

And while there's always been Marilyn Monroe and Elvis Presley and even wacky Ernie Kovacs with his Nairobi Trio and its weird apelike performers, there's also been Audrey Hepburn, Doris Day, and Pat Boone, though he's admittedly a little way out when he sings "Ain't That a Shame?" Walt Kelly gets a little wicked sometimes in Pogo (his character Simple J. Malarkey is clearly a daring satire on Senator Joseph P. McCarthy); but there's always been, for balance, Blondie's common sense when she reproves the bumbling Dagwood, and on Sunday, in striking colors, the armored bravery and perpetual trials of Prince Valiant. They've read about upcoming "adult" Westerns, such as *Have Gun, Will Travel* with the crisis-ridden,

Shakespeare-quoting gunfighter Paladin. But there's never been anything neurotic about Marshal Matt Dillon or Sheriff Will Kane. It has all averaged out. And *average* has always been good.

Nonetheless, their culture has been moving slowly away from Mom and Dad. The days of "togetherness" and "do it your-self," when they all gathered 'round to put up the new wallpaper or solve that mammoth puzzle picture of Old Faithful, have lately seemed a little distant. Maybe this is normal as they get ready to graduate from high school. There are two southern Kings making trouble. One of them, Elvis Presley, is a monarch of rock 'n' roll. He sings of unreliable hound dogs and inconstant women, not the treacle of doggies in the window. The other King speaks in hypnotic cadences about overcoming racial bar-riers. They're accustomed to preachers like Norman Vincent Peale with his positive thinking and do-it-yourself religiosity, but they've never heard a preacher talk like King before. Both Kings know how to cast a spell.

Mom and Dad seem mildly anxious about all that is going on in their kids' lives. Things are just so different, what will be left for the kids to experience when they grow up? These days they seem to have their own music, their own hot rods, and even their own allowances. Now that they have disposable income, there are movies just for them, such as *Bwana Devil*, where the spears seem to fly off the screen, and the 3-D *Crea-ture from the Black Lagoon*, which they saw with Polaroid dark glasses, and even drive-in movies, which their elders suspect are "passion pits" because of the necking that goes on in some of those old jalopies. Dick Clark is ever clean-cut and all-American, and the kids know he is playing their kind of music just for them.

No need to take this too far. They are still largely of one mind with their parents—if Mom and Dad and Eisenhower are worried about outer space, then they are, too. Though no one would ever say they have a different mindset altogether, they are starting to acquire, just maybe, apart from their elders and their betters, minds of their own.

Magazines Have Always Been Mad

Members of this class were born in 1952 and graduated from high school in 1970. If they went on to college—and they could do so far more easily now with the support of National Defense Student Loans and Pell Grants—they would be in the class of 1974.

Members of their class include sportscaster Bob Costas; actor, dancer, and singer Patrick Swayze; and comedienne Roseanne Barr.

John Dewey, Carl Jung, Maria Montessori, Evita Perón, and FDR's beloved dog Fala have always been dead.

Mindset List

1. Planes have always been jet-powered and submarines atomic-powered.

2. The United States Census Bureau has always asked about the number of television sets in a household.

3. They have always driven their parents nuts with "cruelty" jokes: "Other than that, Mrs. Lincoln, how was the play?"

4. George Jorgensen has always been Christine.

5. Dave Brubeck has always been cool.

6. Since they were second graders, the U.S. flag has had fifty stars.

7. There has always been a link between cancer and smoking.

8. Word on the street is that once they head off to college, a first name is all they will need to crash at someone's pad as long as they like.

9. Americans have always been able to wake up to the *Today* show.

10. "First-strike" and "getting to first base" have always involved more than just baseball.

11. "Acid" has always been something more than corrosive.

12. The United States has never occupied Japan but has always had a hydrogen bomb.

13. Margarine has always looked just like butter.

14. Trusting no one over thirty, their generation's anthem has always included "I hope I die before I'm old."

15. When they were eleven, they had to learn a five-digit zip code as part of their address.

16. Computers rather than human operators have always been routing long-distance phone calls, allowing most people to pick up the phone and dial anywhere in the country.

17. As they've gotten more and more rambunctious, their parents could always, thank goodness, pop a Valium.

18. Grandparents have always blamed Dr. Spock for fostering coddled children and rebellious adolescents.

19. They might have done the Twist at their eleventh birthday party.

20. Their teenage years have seen headlines about giving a Head Start to the Other America.

21. Long before they shaved, they saw Rapid Shave do the job well on sandpaper.

22. They investigated their first teen crushes with the help of tarot cards and Ouija boards.

23. Some Weathermen didn't deal with the weather at all, and firehoses in the deep South weren't just for fires.

24. The stories have always been true but the names have always been changed to protect the innocent . . . Dum de dum dum.

25. For a few years parents hoped that the popular Etch A Sketch might bring out the artist in their child.

26. Elvis has always been planning to quit the movies.

27. They were between their junior and senior year in high school on that July morning when President Nixon announced that "this

was the greatest week in the history of the world since Creation," as he welcomed U.S. astronauts back to Earth after their successful journey to the moon.

28. "Stoned" and "laid" have always been passive verbs.

29. The Rat Pack gets less cool every year.

30. The skinny British model Twiggy has become an international female icon, a dramatic contrast to the full-figured Marilyn Monroe, who died in 1962.

31. Bob Dylan's use of an electric guitar at the Newport Jazz Festival has disillusioned them, just as Shoeless Joe Jackson once betrayed their grandparents.

32. They've seen their older sisters head off to college complete with miniskirts, go-go boots, and a container of pills that looks like a telephone dial.

33. Sensory excess must be good for you if Dr. Timothy Leary at Harvard says so.

34. They've grown up being advised to listen to the warm and to remember that groovy is better than greedy.

35. No matter what you are praying for, collectively asking God for assistance during school hours has always aroused a devil of a controversy.

36. For them, Johnny Carson has always been the king of late night.

37. Their parents have always had the chance to say the secret word and win a hundred dollars from a duck with a mustache.

38. Some Brillo boxes come in silk screens, while paintings of Campbell's soup cans are a rarefied art form.

39. Beatles has always been spelled with an "a," and the folks just don't get it.

40. They've grown up in the last days of the gay and eligible young bachelor.

41. Richard Burton and Elizabeth Taylor, either singly or together, have always behaved badly.

42. Catholics may enjoy steak any day of the week.

43. Batman has gotten very arch and campy, and Spider-Man has always been a nerd.

44. Older brothers might have sneaked pot back home from either San Francisco Bay or Cam Rahn Bay.

45. They've never *not* had Nixon to kick around.

46. "Hanging out" and "sleeping around" have become reasonable alternatives to dating.

47. All through high school they've heard Bob Dylan, Jane Fonda, Joan Baez, and the Byrds allegedly giving aid and comfort to the enemy, with their strongly worded opposition to the war in Vietnam.

48. Now that they're about to enter college, they've heard that the girls say yes to love and the boys say no to war.

49. When they were infants, Grandpa, showing off his Hydraglide power steering and radial tires, gave them a ride in his big new Imperial.

50. The times and the words they are a-changin', and the womyn in Amerika are getting angry.

* * * *

We often forget, as we think about those Americans born in the early fifties and destined to grow up in the riotous sixties, that not everyone in that age group turned on, tuned in, and dropped out. We likewise fail to recall that even if they did, they were once young kids. They grew up in the America of Ozzie and Harriet and of Ike; of older siblings whose most daring behavior might have been to take off their shoes for a sock hop. They were the very image of earnest and smiling innocence. Within several short years they would look very different—not just older but also prematurely knowledgeable about the world and its potential for darkness. They would turn to self-styled prophets and poets for answers to a social and political milieu that, to them, would seem unacceptably hypocritical, unjust, repressive, staid, and violent (even if, at times, the violence was of their own creation). These kids, content to look young, eight or so years later will want to look old, with scruffy beards, long hair, and faces looking stoned and disillusioned and far away. It has long been an American tradition that children grow up and write their own verses to songs already written by their elders. But these kids will want to grow up and write their own, entirely new, songs. And they would be loud and angry, too—either that or hootenanny sweet but firmly lodging a protest against the world into which they had been born. Look at these kids one way, and you see the typical adorable unknowing; look at them another way, and you see the faces of the crowd that would become a new American archetype: the impossible-to-understand teenager who has, in one way or another, been with us ever since.

* * * *

Eighteen years ago the class of 1970 was born into a Norman Rockwell scene, a cozy family with a working dad, a stay-at-home mom, and several brothers and sisters. It wasn't long, however, before the Norman Rockwell paintings became museum artifacts, and the familiar weekly *Saturday Evening Post* covers were replaced by the rude and subversive grin of Alfred E. Neuman asking "What, me worry?" *Mad* magazine quickly became the symbol of youthful rebellion best exemplified by all the fifth graders who hid it inside their textbook so they could surreptitiously read it in class. They felt a little like their beloved Spider-Man, who had his own "official" life as a nerd but a far more glamorous hidden one as a comic-book superhero. When parents or teachers caught them with *Mad*, these authority figures were quick to confiscate such childish and satirical material, sometimes only to recover it later for their own secret (if hypocritical) enjoyment and confirmation of their worst fears: the kids had discovered a new role model—skeptical, prone to ridiculing the older generation, quick to sniff out contradictions between what adults say and what they do. They had to face the fact that their youngsters were now reading about Darnold Duck, who saw the absurdity of having to wear gloves just because he was the only Disney character with three fingers and who wanted to murder all the other characters; and the disrespectable G.I. Schmoe, a braggart who boasted of his all-American heroics to luscious Asian broads. This was pretty shocking stuff. Little did they know then that much worse was coming.

Yet for most of the class, their first ten years were uneventful. To be sure, the fifteen-minute nightly news programs brought home the occasional ugly violence from southern cities where there were frequent conflicts between local firehose-wielding authorities and outside "troublemakers" who were trying to change things too fast. By the time they were thirteen, they could watch a war unfold before their eyes in Vietnam, with live news coverage of rice-paddy shoot-outs in places with very foreign-sounding names such as Hue (for some reason pronounced "Whey") and Khe Sahn. But their folks have always tried to shield them from such ugliness. After all, the new medium of television was supposed to educate and entertain them. Long before the fighting in 'Nam, the kids had had Winky Dink with his magic slate and weekly secret codes, along with *Zoo Parade* with Marlin Perkins and his serene zebras and his ravenous hippos, to distract them. By this time TV sets were as common in American households as radios had once been.

Whether they were watching Captain Kangaroo with his gentle pal Mr. Greenjeans or Douglas Edwards with the nightly quarter-hour news of rioting in Venezuela, they grew up with the huge console TV as the focus of the living room, with three or four networks that offered programming all day, signing off at midnight with the national anthem. Then the boring test pattern ran until about seven the next morning. The size and scope of the console gradually expanded to reflect the family's status as it incorporated the radio, the phonograph, the reel-to-reel tape recorder, and, occasionally, the full bar.

As youngsters, they got their preparation for kindergarten from Miss Frances at the Ding Dong Schoolhouse and dreamed of the chance to someday sit in the Peanut Gallery on *The Howdy Doody Show*, where they risked getting sprayed by Clarabell's seltzer bottle, which was usually aimed at Buffalo Bob. (If Dad was around, he watched it only if the fetching Princess Summerfall Winterspring was on.) Educational TV stations were starting to broadcast, and rumor had it that Fran, that genial girl with her puppet pals Kukla and Ollie, would soon be televised in color, but most kids wouldn't be able to enjoy it that way unless they visited a wealthy friend whose TV set could display the NBC peacock in its full glory.

Mom made sure the TV lamp was on so that they wouldn't hurt their eyes—she wanted to be certain that they stayed out of range of those damaging cathode rays. On special nights they set up TV trays and ate fried chicken or Salisbury steak from Swanson aluminum plates and watched *Disneyland*, with its four separate "lands," or *Bonanza*, with the Cartwright brothers on their sprawling ranch.

* * * *

After graduating from high school, the class of 1970 could look back on a feeling of security and comfort, despite the burgeoning violence on the tube or the obscure warnings that just maybe Frontier Land or Fantasy Land are simply neighborhoods in a "vast wasteland." As teens entering junior high school, they awoke one day to discover that their parents were just a little afraid of them. The folks weren't comfy with the new music, the new language, and the new style. Suddenly *Mad* magazine seemed the least of the distortions and discontinuities. Parents might have been glad to believe that Alfred E. Neuman was the extent of the rebellion and wished they could go back to the good old days when confiscating *Mad* ended the troubles. Throughout the country there was constant talk about gaps— missile, credibility, and generation. Young people only a little older than class members were "crashing" with friends and going to "happenings." Parents of these older children reported traumatic stories: for example, their college kids have been explaining to them that they'd better start swimming or they'll sink like a stone, and that "freedom" was just another word for nothing left to lose. The differences between males and females were growing ever more unclear. It was not unusual for parents to see women whose hair was shorter than their sixteen-year-old son's, and men whose hair was longer than Mom's. Parents of the class of '70 began to wonder how their own children would turn out in just a few years. They began to worry and fuss, or sometimes just shake their heads in resignation or disgust.

But some friends with older kids were more encouraging; many of the kids, now working and studying hard, weren't all that different from how they were ten or fifteen years ago. For them, the girls and the boy are still dependably different. That's a relief.

But anxieties and estrangement aside, and notwithstanding novel and frightening lifestyles, life has remained generally pretty good. In large numbers families have moved to the suburbs, and Dad has become a pretty handy guy, building bookshelves for the stereophonic components and installing a new patio. He really could "do-it-yourself," and one of the first things he did was cover the old hardwood floors with wall-to-wall carpeting so he and Mom could finally invite the neighbors in. A little later, they would hear that young people called "hippies" thought carpeting was unnatural, materialistic, and invidiously middle-class. Mom was learning all sorts of new tricks in the kitchen—amazing new international treats like quiche and fondue—from female chefs like Dione Lucas and Julia Child, who had their own television shows. Prompted by a bit of commercial advice, Mom discovered that you could dress up anything by adding a few cans of Campbell's cream of mushroom soup.

Playing in the house was pretty much forbidden, so the kids were sent out to play until the streetlights came on, but nearby enough to hear when Mom called you—and don't slam the screen door on the way out. Members of the class of '70 grew up with Sunday afternoon family dinners that cut into their playtime, but since most families ate at about the same time, they could just put the game on hold. On Sundays tables were set with matching china and glassware acquired from supermarket and gas station promotions, one piece each week. Amy Vanderbilt's new book on etiquette explained how to set the table correctly, in addition to offering detailed advice on personal conduct and decorum. Just as it was amazing what could be done with a creative Campbell's soup recipe, it was equally astounding how much you could get with S&H Green Stamps. On special occasions, Victor Borge's Rock Cornish Hens and Mom's green bean casserole with fried onions provided the perfect meal for company. Oleomargarine tasted like real butter, and it came from the store already yellow; Mom no longer had to put the white stuff in a bag with a food coloring pill and massage it.

So by then did it really matter that Junior and Betty were starting to listen to deafening music the words of which Mom and Dad couldn't understand, or that the folks had read about such things as light shows and pot, or that " in" had become a radical new suffix for everything from sit-ins to be-ins and that their own kids in the class of 1970 might someday participate in such shenanigans? The Beatles sang "Let It Be"—those words the parents *could* understand—but surely their own children wouldn't go to college just to "be" but to *do*, perhaps medicine or law or business or teaching. Wouldn't they?

In the meantime, the house had been slowly filling up with the new stereophonic sound of high fidelity, living presence, and dynamic decibels. Dad was so proud of his technical proficiency with receivers, amps, and pre-amps that he constantly made family and guests sit in one special spot so they could hear his new LP of jet planes, locomotives, or drums that made the sound seem to go across the room from one speaker to the other. He said it was like the new theater experience and called it "Cinerama for sound." The kids might have seemed a bit bored by all that. And when everybody was gone, he put his new "Sing Along with Mitch" LP back on.

If at times a bit boring, the world also seemed safe, at least for the most part. Word was circulating that there was some connection between smoking and lung cancer, but the cigarette companies were making things safer with gas-trap and charcoal filters on new king-size cigarettes. It was not hard to imagine the kids taking up the habit, since everybody smoked and every coffee table was equipped with the fancy silver Ronson lighter (a favorite birthday or Christmas gift) and ashtray. In further progress toward deliverance from peril, the arrival of the Salk and Sabin vaccines meant that they no longer had to fear polio or adjust vacation plans in order to avoid travel to areas where there were summer outbreaks.

The nation has been not only prosperous—less than forty years after the Great Depression—but also growing. The addition of Alaska and Hawaii to the union prompted a redesign of the flag. Members of the class of '70 have grown up with the constant challenge of rather overcrowded schools and the need to construct new ones. Families have been growing rapidly, and everybody has been moving to the "country" and pushing the limits of the suburbs. There was a slight chance that in the suburban schools they might encounter students of other races for the first time. Whether the kids were bused from other schools (which had happened in only a few areas) or came from minority families who were starting to move into new northern neighborhoods, the makeup of these "country" communities was starting to change.

But this was nothing like the schools in the cities that they had left behind, where it was common to mix kids of different backgrounds and races. Some of these suburban communities actually had racial restrictions on who could live there. But Mom and Dad didn't talk about these problems. Even so, college-age kids, just a few years older than the class of 1970, were making a stink about them as more examples of the "racist" and two-faced character of the oldsters, who claimed they were moving to the 'burbs for cleaner air but may also have been motivated by a desire to avoid the influx of upwardly mobile black families now moving into formerly all-white neighborhoods. Class member Roseanne Barr grew up working-class Jewish in Salt Lake City, having to hide her religion from Mormons—just another example, their older siblings might say, of adult hypocrisy and repression.

* * * *

Education—especially science and math—has been the topic of constant conversation ever since the Russians surprised the world with a man-made satellite in space. When members of the class were five years old, they along with everyone else went out in the yard at night to see if they could spot Sputnik circling the planet or faintly hear its incessant beeping. Their parents wondered how the Soviets had beaten us and what other surprises this godless enemy power might have in store. For a long time, the United States couldn't seem to get anything off the ground and into space. Every effort, it seems, blew up on the launch pad, and class members may recall reading in the derisory morning paper that the United States had launched a "Pfffffftnik." By the time they had started school, the Mercury missions were beginning and the space race was on in earnest. At least we had brought Ham the chimp back from an early launch into orbit, unlike the Russians, who left Laika the dog to die up there. When the kids were nine, they may have stayed home to watch the TV coverage of Alan Shepard's fifteen minutes in space, holding their breath while the retrieval team tried to open the hatch to get him out of the space capsule when it landed in the ocean. He made it! Whew!

For the class of 1970 the best part of all this excitement was that, in the name of national defense, the government was coming up with financial support programs to help students attend college so that Americans would have the brainpower in science and math to beat the Russians in the future. Their parents soon enough told them that now anyone could go to college and that they were, darn it, expected to do so, too. In the privacy of their hearts class members might have wondered what the scoffing, raucous Janis Joplin and Jim Morrison would have thought of such nonnegotiable demands, but in general they agreed and were about to enter college in record numbers. After all, thanks to vinyl they can take Janis and Jim with them, and this is precisely what they are planning to do, hoping they don't draw a classical-music nerd as a roommate.

The good life on the patio and the thick carpets notwithstanding, as their kids have started to move up in the grades, parents have become more nervous about the increasing availability of atomic weapons, whose terrifying mushroom clouds they've marveled at on television. The fact that we had the hydrogen bomb was reassuring—but what if we have to use it? After all, the Soviets had one too! A famous acronym was "MAD"—Mutual Assured Destruction—and once again parents have started longing for *Mad* magazine: at least *that* "Mad" was relatively harmless.

There was also a lot of talk about the moral decline of the nation and the disappearance of all standards in the country. As these parents looked back on earlier times, when the kids were watching Phineas T. Bluster trying to corrupt Doodyville, they wondered whether they were right to feel so comfy. Even back then, after all, crooks seemed to be running some of the cities, and they had watched racketeers repeatedly "take the Fifth" on TV about how the unions are run. Despite the fall of Senator Joseph McCarthy, the fear that Communists may have infiltrated our national institutions has remained, and even President Eisenhower's top aide may have once been bribed with a fancy coat. The most popular quiz shows turned out to have been fixed, high-living sports figures were being glamorized, doctors were taking kickbacks, and disc jockeys were being investigated for accepting payola from record companies to play certain records. Rumors were widespread that politicians were hiring ghostwriters to craft their speeches. When the kids were starting junior high, *Time* magazine raised the question "Is God Dead?"—yet another challenge to the status quo.

While communities were debating the need for bomb shelters, the big moral argument was about who would be allowed into them if they had one. People understood that there was no room for second place in a competition built on mutually assured destruction. Parents were concerned about how much radioactive waste from the atmosphere was in the milk the kids were drinking. When the kids were seven, there were no cranberries on the Thanksgiving table, since the cranberry bogs might have become contaminated with nuclear residue.

* * * *

Soon enough a different sort of fallout began to hit their own households, and the crisis seemed no farther away than their own living rooms or upstairs bedrooms. As the kids moved ever closer to high school, the quality of the dinner conversations with the family began to decline. Things were changing too fast for their heroic, World War II–era parents. If the family was fortunate enough to have a second phone upstairs "for the kids," they started calling their friends at night to complain about the edgy discussions regarding hair, language, music, money, and the length of the skirts. Parents were hearing reports about college deans cowering before their fearsome charges, pleading with the kids to "just stick with the booze" as a way of inducing them to avoid drugs; and of new philosophies from radical professors suggesting that sex and drugs, and lots of both, were always good for expanding one's consciousness. The worst-case scenarios described by parents with children a few years older seemed to be coming true in their own households, as well. Where would it all end—the happenings, the LSD, the protests, even calling the president of the United States a war criminal?

While parents had been trying to keep the class of 1970 safe from harm, they now believed the kids were trying to blow their own minds with their new music. Music has changed, and all the bands seem angry at something. The ubiquitous piano in the living room has been replaced by the electric guitar in the basement or the garage. The mellow sounds of the older generation's favorite tenors, baritones, and girl groups have been relegated to Sundays on the radio or to those stations that philosophically oppose rock 'n' roll; for a while veterans of the big band era tried rather ridiculously to croon Elvis hits on *Your Hit Parade*. (No doubt Alfred E. Neuman would have beamed his wickedly lackadaisical smile on that!)

Music has taken the once-lowly—but now subversive—guitar in opposite directions. If it's not rock 'n' roll with the Beatles and Motown, then it's folk music and hootenannies with Peter, Paul and Mary and the Kingston Trio, with Bob Dylan somewhere in between. All of it expressed opposition to something—community standards and family values, or the government and the Vietnam war, or ticky-tacky houses and lifestyles. Modern "riffing" jazz challenged the melodic jazz standards. Then there was the just plain weird, represented by the falsetto Tiny Tim and his bashful bride, Miss Vicki. White groups offering soft interpretations of rhythm and blues hits gave way to the original black groups on Dick Clark's *American Bandstand*. Insisting that "that's not music," parents everywhere condemned it all, describing it as a lot of noise that all sounds alike. It's not that the parents were total squares. Dean Martin singing "Everybody Loves Somebody Sometime" or even Ray Charles with his contemporary sound: now there, at least, was music! And if you wanted rebellion, these parents might well ask, why not stick to the Rat Pack, where the likes of Sinatra and Martin and Sammy Davis Jr. could celebrate the joys of booze and chicks? Yet with every passing year the Rat Pack seemed less cool than the year before.

Alas, as members of the class of 1970 were turning into teenagers, their parents could have prayed that they'd find an old copy of *'Twixt 12 and 20*. In it Pat Boone—twice as popular as Elvis according to certain polls of teens in the late '50s—wrote of the joys and problems of these exciting years. Their parents would be glad to see them reading such wholesome literature from a singer once popular with teens not so many years earlier. But such prayers would have generally gone unanswered.

On the other hand, whatever the prayers of their parents, there was an infinitely greater likelihood that the kids had gotten themselves a red hunting hat to go along with their copy of *Catcher in the Rye*, which their friends had all been reading and which they were loath to share with parents or teachers, not realizing that those parents and teachers may have already read the book. It became the mythic creed for a new tribe in formation, an increasingly disaffected social unit—the teen—that could continue to influence American culture for years to come. On one fine day members of the class of 1970 apparently found out that they were a new phenomenon: the teenager. They were smart, advanced, sensual, hip, weird (in a good way), and, above all, authentic. They were not, and never would be, like those "phonies" that Holden Caulfield skewered and despised. Somehow everyone now knew, as the class of '70 was about to embark for college, that while there had been teens before in the chronological sense, there had never before been *teens* as a type—until now.

* * * *

As these young people have started to develop their personal philosophies in a confusing world, Kahlil Gibran's *The Prophet* and Rod McKuen's *Listen to the Warm*, published in the late

1960s, have uplifted, inspired, and stimulated them. Gibran, a Lebanese philosopher and poet who died nearly forty years earlier in the American Northeast, has enchanted class members with his twenty-six poetic essays about love, eating and drinking, buying and selling, sorrow, and much else. He was something of a mystic, who acknowledged that his meaning was often enigmatic. Class members were enraptured with cryptic lines like "Beauty is eternity gazing at itself in a mirror," and "Love knows not its own depth until the hour of parting." However vague this might have sounded to their parents, for this rebellious, college-bound generation it was Khalil who knows best—not Father. McKuen was an American poet and songwriter whose poems were equally fuzzy but oracular. He said you must not only feel the warm, but also listen to it as a way out of darkness and self-centeredness; and that "facts," such as those of the new plastics industry that the perplexed Dustin Hoffman was urged to join in *The Graduate*, should give way to an imagery that clothes such mundane matters in the spiritual robes of poetry. If Bob Dylan was right that the times are a-changin'—and by now it seems clear that he was—then the huge popularity of Gibran and McKuen were indisputable signs that the whole world was shifting toward something else, still indefinable—somewhat like the meaning of McKuen's verse or Gibran's philosophy.

Even before the popular advent of Middle Eastern philosophers and contemporary American poets like Ginsberg and Kerouac, the worldview of this class had changed dramatically on a Friday afternoon in November 1963, when they were in sixth grade. The assassination of President John F. Kennedy was the most traumatic public experience of their young lives. They had seen pictures of the nice, old, bald grandfather figure their folks called Ike, but Kennedy reminded them of their still-youthful uncle, and he was the only president they had been intensely aware of; he had little kids and was on television all the time, a Cold War Prince Valiant who charmingly called Cuba "Cuber." The folks had been scared at times—especially when the Americans and Soviets had been eyeball to eyeball over "Cuber" the year before—but they had listened to the president whom some of them referred to as "Jack," and he had reassured them they were okay. Soviet premier Nikita Khrushchev had apparently taken his missiles and gone home. Yet now, right there on television, Kennedy was dead; and then the man who shot him was himself shot while they watched. Class members may well have memories, seven years later, of what the living room looked like after a long weekend of wrenching TV: a disaster area of empty Coke cans and discarded TV dinners, some with the meat loaf and gravy still sitting there. Most people, of any age, had been too upset to deal with this domestic catastrophe until after JFK had been buried and a more normal sort of mourning could begin.

As eleven-year-olds, they had little idea of the politics of the times and of what had or had not been accomplished. They just saw their teachers cry and a nation come to a halt and go into silent sadness. They may have curled up with their copy of *Happiness Is a Warm Puppy* to get through it, contemplating the crises of Linus, Lucy, Pigpen, and Snoopy; but their innocence ended early. In that, they were like the nation as a whole.

* * * *

Ever since that terrible day, politics began to work its way into their consciousness, and it emerged as a profoundly unattractive sight. The first president they were aware of was shot, and a year later his successor—an imposing man with a western drawl that was alternately bellowing and reassuring—was campaigning with the terrifying image of a little girl picking a daisy that turned into a bomb blast and a mushroom cloud. Then there was a threatening southern segregationist with surprising support even in the North. The presidential elections of 1964 and 1968 were surrounded by riots and war, preceded by more assassinations of those who stood for what the students believed. If their childhoods were knee-deep in avuncular TV dads such as Ben Cartwright, Ozzie Nelson, and Ward Cleaver, their adolescence has become knee-deep in murdered political martyrs.

Other aspects of their lives were suffering from a radical discontinuity. Mom's been getting out of the kitchen more and more now; she has even found that some of her friends are talking about working at real jobs, and she's beginning to wonder whether she should, too. She has read about the "feminine mystique" and is starting to feel that she can do more in life than wash dishes, cook meals, and wipe noses. Few moms are like the mother of class member Patrick Swayze of Houston; she has a full-time career as a choreographer and dance instructor. If Mom has an older daughter, she may have heard her offspring sermonizing that the personal is political—that politics is a matter not just of voting but also of what we are doing (or not doing) in our daily lives—and now she is also trying to get Mom to at least go to a lecture. The development and FDA approval of Enovid has assured Mom that she has some control over having more children, and members of the class of 1970 have become more than okay with the idea that they would not have to share a room with a younger brother or sister. The only problem was that while Mom and Dad were happy that they could use the Pill, they were less than thrilled that their teenage kids can use it, as well; they are hearing more and more stories about sexual promiscuity becoming common among their kids' age group.

But there was a great deal more to the overall revolt. What had started when class members were three, when Rosa Parks refused to relinquish her seat on a bus to a white man in Alabama, has led to potential revolution everywhere. Schools and public facilities were struggling to desegregate in the South, and northern cities and communities had been told that they would have to change their behavior, too. Now there was talk of modifying the concept of neighborhood schools in order to bus students to other communities, all in the name of something called "racial balance." The colleges they would attend had established new programs to discover and admit talented minority students, either as a part of their mission or because the courts ordered them to. The new emphasis was not just on guaranteed opportunity but also on guaranteed results. A furious Alabama governor would say that such programs come from "pointy-headed intellectuals who can't park their bicycles straight." He might be, soon enough, describing members of the class of '70.

The class of 1970 emerged from graduation as a new force in society. Their parents may have had to persuade them to attend their graduation for the sake of their grandparents. Their friends all knew it was "phony," but they went, too. In record numbers they planned to go on to college, partly because it was one sure way to avoid the draft and fighting *in* the war they were already fighting *against* at home. In their minds, whatever the noble intentions of the United States in fighting Communism in Southeast Asia, it had become a war of white colonial masters against the yellow-skinned wretched of the earth and, hence, morally reprehensible, whatever their parents and more traditionally minded peers in the Young Americans for Freedom may think.

Yet as they prepared to go off to what looked like the *relevant* battlefield of the college campus, the protest movement may have already peaked; the assassinations of Bobby Kennedy and Martin Luther King Jr. two years earlier, and the riots that followed, may have already drained energy from its noisy crest. While the young men still had a chance of being drafted for service, the war seemed to be on the wane (at least President Nixon was withdrawing troops), and the draft was now a lottery, based on the birth dates of men who had registered with the Selective Service. The Chicago Democratic Convention, with its chaotic police riot, was now two years in the past, and Students for a Democratic Society, frequently at the center of protests, dissolved amid shouting and more chaos. The Kent State and Jackson State shootings were fresh and terrible memories.

Their parents were worried about them once again—this time not because of the possibility of political killings or the deafness that would surely result from barbarically loud music— but about their very safety as they headed to college. Whether the campuses were perilous or not, class member Bob Costas was heading to Syracuse University, where he would study sportscasting at the S. I. Newhouse School of Public Communications. Nixon's honeymoon phase was ending—in winding down the war he also seemed to be winding it up, to the predictable accompaniment of jeers from yet more protesters. Meanwhile, American astronauts have landed on the moon. Walter Cronkite, still the most trusted man in America, commented that even the jaded hippies have to get excited about *that*.

The generation that President Lyndon Johnson said was "appointed by history" to do great things was about to be unleashed. Cool Whip, Tang, Velcro, Negro students graduating from Ole Miss, Earth Day, men on the moon, female generals, the Peace Corps: nothing seemed impossible. But first they would have to navigate a college campus without getting shot or zonked out on acid or speed—and they would have to figure out how they could trust those over thirty with whom, in order to fulfill their great destinies, they would surely have to work someday.

There Has Always Been the
Grateful Dead

Members of this class were born in 1965, graduated from high school in 1983, and would graduate from college in 1987.

Members of their class include comedian Chris Rock and actors Sarah Jessica Parker and Robert Downey Jr.

Malcolm X, Alan Freed, and Nat "King" Cole have always been dead.

Mindset List

1. Leaving them as tots with a babysitter, their parents were eager to attend the unclothed annunciation of the Age of Aquarius.

2. They've never needed to worry about being drafted.

3. There has always been an ecology movement, and in first grade they got time off from school to pick up litter.

4. They've always heard cautionary tales about kids who wrecked their lives in druggy communes.

5. They've probably never heard a cigarette ad on the radio.

6. Women have always worn pants.

7. Elected officials have always worn American flag pins on their lapels.

8. "Ethnics" have started thinking blacks got breaks denied to them, and vice versa.

9. Thanks to the glut of children born since World War II, nearly half the country's population is now under thirty.

10. It has never been legal, however "equal," to offer separate facilities based on race.

11. The major social issues of their lifetime have involved the status of women.

12. The baby boom has always been over, the "birth dearth" always on.

13. They have never known an *elected* Snow Belt president.

14. The nation has always been trying to recapture its spirit.

15. The "typical family of four," headed by a working father with a stay-at-home mother and two children, has always been the exception.

16. Maybe Germany and Japan won World War II after all.

17. No bouncing is allowed on the folks' waterbed.

18. Their grandparents, better off financially than their parents ever expect to be, might have spent a vacation or two at some Disneyland for the Devout.

19. They will soon go to college, where they will find that the Sexual Revolution has already graduated.

20. By the time they were in middle school, borrowing money from a loan shark might have been cheaper than borrowing from a bank.

21. They have grown up watching TV shows about nontraditional families that seemed to be happier than their own traditional ones.

22. Their grandparents have always had Medicare.

23. Blacks and whites have always been kissing on TV.

24. They will never see the Beatles in live performance, use a slide rule, or have to wait until age twenty-one in order to vote.

25. Native Americans have always been an acknowledged ethnic group with their own political agenda.

26. Their mothers might have accepted a Tiparillo from a gentleman or come a long way with Virginia Slims.

27. Multicolored jogging suits, dullish earth shoes, and many-flavored juice bars have long been popular.

28. Denim has been used for everything from peace signs to evening jackets to Bible covers.

29. T-shirts have always been proclaiming both the profound and the silly philosophies of the wearer.

30. The audience for rock has always been getting gray at the temples.

31. Looking in vain for the next John, Paul, George, and Ringo, the nation has instead gotten . . . Ziggy Stardust.

32. They may have first heard "fag," "spic," and "spade" from the mellifluous lips of Archie Bunker, and first encountered the F word in a film as uttered by Captain "Painless" Waldowski in *M.A.S.H.*—in a video at home.

33. In fourth grade, when their parents stayed out late on Saturday nights, they sneaked their first taste of the absurd masquerade of the Coneheads and the Czech Brothers' obsessions with "large American breasts."

34. They've always understood the tragic "roots" of American slavery.

35. Long hair has become more the style, even for Dad, with every passing year.

36. Cassius Clay has always been Muhammad Ali, and Lew Alcindor has always been Kareem Abdul-Jabbar.

37. Color TV has become the norm, and thanks to Mr. Dolby, they've never had to listen to hiss on their recordings.

38. There has always been the Grateful Dead.

39. They grew up Ponging their tennis games on a screen.

40. America has always been sliding by on plastic.

41. The Catholic priest has always faced his parishioners at mass on Saturday.

42. There have always been miniskirts, domed stadiums, and Diet Pepsi.

43. As their parents couldn't stop watching Carnac the Magnificent on weeknights and the birthrate has continued to fall, maybe they're lucky to have been born at all.

44. They've grown up with predictions that the country would soon have national health care as a solution to soaring costs and inadequate coverage.

45. Joints (the kind you smoke) have always been part of their birthright.

46. Diaper services have always been going the way of the buggy whip.

47. They've grown up cooking their own after-school snacks in the toaster oven or microwave while waiting for their parents to get home.

48. When they were nine, some of them couldn't understand what exactly a water gate was supposed to keep in or out.

49. Owing to a yellow Big Bird, they were the first class to enter first grade with a confident knowledge of letters and numbers.

50. Commuters in Mustangs, Ramblers, and Beetles have always been starving inner cities of tax revenue.

* * * *

The class of 1983 was only six years old when the Children's Television Workshop gave them a learning boost beyond what they had gotten as preschoolers from Sesame Street, *and this was in the somewhat more advanced program* The Electric Company. *Starring such great artists as Morgan Freeman, Bill Cosby, and Rita Moreno, the show gave the kids added practice in the proper use of words. A wacky superhero named Letterman—who flew around with a football helmet on—battled Spell Binder, the evil conjurer who had a nasty habit of changing and twisting words. The kids have five seconds to read a fast-vanishing word, and a word appeared to challenge their reading skills just before the lightbulb was switched off the program for good that day. Dr. Doolots, a blend of Dr. Doolittle and Groucho Marx, tried to treat his patients with . . . words. And so it went on and on. This program meant a lot to the class of 1983, as they were the first grammar school kids to benefit from it. It was also a hallmark of the decade in which they grew up, for the 1970s were at once innovative and fragmented; so it figures that the class of '83 would get a TV show that was maddeningly clever even as it helped keep them occupied in homes increasingly likely to be affected by divorce or families in which both parents worked. And like much else in that decade, what was creative was also disposable. By the time they were twelve,* The Electric Company *had left the air as a regular part of the weekday.*

* * * *

As the class of 1983 is graduating from high school and on its way to college, its members have a sense of disappointment.

Although they have been among the most privileged of American younger generations—like the other generations that grew up post-Depression and postwar—they have also matured in a time more cynical and less idealistic, less hopeful, and less prosperous. The previous generation sounded a certain trumpet, even if it sounded like rock 'n' roll. The class of 1983, like many others in their country, has been in retreat. Unlike their older siblings or cousins, who were born a decade before, they could be forgiven for thinking that they've missed everything good and caught everything bad. It's as though the class of 1983 missed the party but went straight to the hangover.

As they have moved into forming their own sexual identities, and are about to head off to university for some real fun, they're hearing about something called AIDS, an often-fatal disease acquired through sex and liable to make you regret you had ever had it. Those in the generation before got their sex free of consequences. There was every excuse made for having lots of it, including the mystical transformation, in bed, of peace to replace war. But what was liberation for the previous bunch is, for the class of 1983, the deadly price of screwing around. Indeed, more worrisome is genital herpes, a sexually transmitted disease that is more prevalent than AIDS, particularly among heterosexuals.

The members of the generation before enjoyed a Golden Age of capitalism—however much they might have liked to say they were fans of Mao or Che—while the class of 1983 has been doomed to hear their worried parents talk about something called "stagflation," in which the economy stagnates and the price of everything soars. It has confounded the economists and prompted their parents to pull out their now widely available plastic cards in order to buy now because everyone knows

that the price will be going up. When class members were in the
fourth grade, they may have happened upon Walter Cronkite
one evening, and he presented to them a preternaturally calm
and balding president smoking a pipe and sporting a WIN button. Their parents may have explained to them that WIN meant
Whip Inflation Now, and that the man wearing the button was
not a winner, because he had never been elected. By the time
they were fourteen, their folks could quote a famous comedian
who said that interest rates, in the name of WINning, were so
high that it would be cheaper to borrow money from the local
loan shark than from the local bank.

It seems all their lives they've been living in a country trying to get its spirit back. Woody Allen, who says he's not afraid
to die but just doesn't want to be there when it happens, gives
voice to the jitters of many. All their lives they've been warned
about an America with limits, inhabiting a planet with too
many people and too many toxins. Ten when the Vietnam War
ended, they've heard countless sad stories either from their
grandparents who told them that America had never lost a war
before, or from young contemporaries who passed on tales of
twentysomethings returning from 'Nam with Japanese cameras
and the latest stereo equipment along with drug addictions,
lost limbs, and postwar syndromes that woke them up screaming in the night. They don't remember a lot about the Watergate scandal, as they were only nine when it resulted in the
resignation of President Nixon, but it has never escaped their
awareness that this was not their grandparents' or even their
parents' president of the United States. Even Hoover never had
to resign from office, and now people are giving even curmud-
geonly old Harry Truman some grudging respect. Nixon has
none at all.

This isn't to say that the previous generation didn't have its own troubles, what with the draft card burnings and the murders of Jack Kennedy, his brother Bobby, and Martin Luther King Jr. But members of that generation, it seems, were world-beaters. Grown-ups seemed afraid of them. No one seems afraid of the class of 1983. It's as though everyone indulged during the 1960s, and now the bill has come due, and they have been drafted, if that's still the right word in these days of volunteer armies, into paying it along with everyone else.

* * * *

When class members were born, the decade of the sixties was still fairly tame. Lyndon Johnson was enjoying the bloom of popularity, and the country seemed to share his aspirations to extend untold national blessings to everyone in a Great Society. He had defeated Senator Barry Goldwater in 1964 because Goldwater seemed dangerously ready to expand the war in Vietnam, while Johnson seemed more measured and reasonable. That was then. By the time they were getting ready to start school, the war had expanded to the point where one national magazine called it a "fourth branch of government." The national consensus about civil rights and income sharing was over. Richard Nixon had become president because he said he had a "secret plan" to end the war, but no one had listened when he also said we needed to "win the peace." Hence, the war, along with the country's divisions about it, was raging on. The National Guard shot kids who were demonstrating in Ohio, some of whom weren't even protesting the war, and half the country didn't seem all that sorry about it. Disillusionment about the country's future rose along with the prices that were depleting personal incomes.

As they were leaving the world of toddlers and about to become young school kids, marriage had become about as fashionable as corsets in a time when even brassieres were being shed. Divorce was as "in" as bell bottoms. Splits during this era included the parents of class member Robert Downey Jr., who at age five appeared as a sick puppy in his father's absurdist underground comedy *Pound*. The parents of another class member, Sarah Jessica Parker, moved from Ohio to New York so she could study creative performance; young Sarah was starring onstage in *Annie* at the age of twelve and then in the network sitcom *Square Pegs*. Indeed, it would have been common for class members to have dozed in their cribs when their parents, married in haste in the roiling sixties, decided to split up, as though they had gone from the nude *Hair* singers announcing the Age of Aquarius straight to the court where the judge announced their divorce. Mom would probably have raised them, but she would also have worked outside the home. This was a product of both newly born women's lib and the necessity for two incomes in inflationary times. They would have been the first American generation to be raised partly by day care centers, which were springing up everywhere. Color TVs, garbage disposals, and revolutionary new "radar ranges"—whose microwaves were suspected of frying their future—would have been near-universal in their everyday world. They were more likely to live in the suburbs than in the cities, and were more likely to live in suburbs in Florida, Texas, or California than those in New York, Massachusetts, or Illinois. When they let themselves into an empty house after school, they became the first generation to entertain themselves with a videotape; they might have heard the F word for the first time in a movie one afternoon while they were watching *M.A.S.H.*—one of the first films to be available in VHS and Beta formats.

Though *The Brady Bunch* and *The Partridge Family* were off national television before class members finished elementary school, they grew up seeing those shows in syndication and would have noted that as a "blended" family the Bradys were hardly abnormal, and that the long hair and bubble-gum pop of the Partridges suggested that lengthy locks no longer meant "not nice" or "extremely dangerous." That still didn't satisfy the growing millions of Americans who were alienated because of their own outmoded views, so by the time these kids were in grammar school, they heard a grouchy if soft-hearted blue-collar worker named Archie rue the day that "fags" and "spics" had started taking over the land. He regarded his own son-in-law's long hair as foreign. "Meathead" seemed to Archie a far more disturbing figure than the long-haired but squeaky-clean Keith Partridge did to the young members of the class of '83. It might have seemed that Archie was the still-strong past while they were the still-helpless future.

They have grown up with their Etch A Sketch drawing boards, Easy Bake Ovens (perfect for turning out mini chocolate cakes), and Nerf Balls. They have disturbed the quiet of a summer afternoon with their ear-shattering Big Wheels. Mom endured can after can of sugar-free Tab until someone told her the artificial sweetener might be cancerous and that it's better to have a few too many pounds than too few cells. They might have been driven about in a wide variety of cars, from Trans-Ams (especially if Dad had left Mom and put in an application for permanent adolescence) to AMC Pacers (pregnant women on roller skates, as they were called) or even flimsy Fiats imported from Italia. They may have diagnosed Dad or Mom with their new Fisher-Price Doctor's Kits, complete with light-blue plastic stethoscopes.

A little later in their young lives they might have helped Mom make fondue with chocolate or cheese in one of the multiple fondue sets the family had received as gifts. And somewhat later than that they would have asked their Magic 8 Balls whether they would end up marrying Rod Stewart or Shaun Cassidy. They would have to decide how to wear their hair: spiked or short or permed or feathered or layered or frosted. Role models included Rod Stewart's shag or Farrah Fawcett's mane or (after the 1976 Winter Olympics) the Dorothy Hamill bob. They would need to hold their portable tape recorders up to the radio in order to record a song. The tape-driven Commodore 64 offered a preview of how computers might come into the home and do more than just help banks keep track of checks and companies keep up with files. The more brainy ones would spend hours trying to solve a Rubik's Cube. They've worn Dr. Scholl's sandals in summer and moon boots in winter. Eight-tracks offer great sound, but then so do cassettes, and that's what they'll be taking to college with them.

* * * *

They have grown up in a frustrated and furious land. Racial segregation in restaurants, schools, and polling places has never been legal. But the TV has often shown angry young black people with Afros who said that even President Lyndon Johnson, who pushed through the country's first civil rights legislation, was not doing enough. They claimed the whole system was fixed against them—though on television the class of '83 has mostly seen blacks in sitcoms, their anger was sheathed in humor and moderated by buffoonery. Blacks lagged severely behind in nearly every category of the nation's blessings—the sort of point that the influential and favorite grandfather of class member Chris Rock might make in his edgy, home-truth sermons. Ghettoes have continued to fester and simmer. Class members were three when Dr. King was killed. When they were about nine, they may have heard something about the violent exploits of the Symbionese Liberation Army (SLA) and the kidnapping of Patty Hearst, and then, when they were twelve, they learned about Kunta Kinte, the horrifically mistreated but determined-to-survive ancestor of Alex Haley, whose *Roots* became the first big TV miniseries. The series, it appears, opened the eyes even of racists to the shame of slavery and the need to know who one is by knowing who one's ancestors were. But otherwise the great book and series have solved nothing, for while one can legislate against legal discrimination, there is no easy solution to the problem of economic injustice. Meanwhile, no black leader inspires them in the way that Dr. King inspired their older brothers and sisters.

Women have been likewise exasperated and angry. They have always demanded equal pay for equal work and insisted on no discrimination based on their gender, but the reality is more complicated. Should female soldiers be allowed in combat situations? Should women be firefighters and be hired for dangerous construction jobs? Should they become just like men and have the same rights to frank sexual declarations? But then if they do, doesn't that mean that men won't take them seriously as professionals? What will really happen if, as the commercial puts it, a woman should accept a plastic-tipped minicigar called a Tiparillo from a "gentleman"? Should the women's movement join forces with blacks and American Indians, who have started their own American Indian Movement (AIM). Or should they, well aware that many black and Indian leaders are otherwise sexist men, focus on their own interests? Is the women's movement about increasing women's power or limiting men's?

Have women really, as the Virginia Slims commercial puts it, come a long way, baby, or is that just another example of how the system rips people off by flattering them? Is heterosexual love a vibrant emotion shared by equals, or—as such radical women's groups as Coyote and Redstockings have maintained—is it an institutional trap? Was Eve framed? Do women need men like a fish needs a bicycle, as some feminists have said? At times these discussions have grown increasingly strident.

All their lives members of the class of 1983 have been surrounded by these vexing questions, even if they haven't always understood them. As the class of '83 begins to move toward adulthood, their mothers and aunts aver that none of these questions has truly been answered. When class members were five, women declared, via the National Organization for Women, that they wanted liberation NOW. The Equal Rights Amendment, or ERA, which would constitutionally outlaw discrimination based on gender, seemed ready to pass, but then pesky questions were raised about the larger implications that could result in a flood of lawsuits. The whole thing has now been shelved. "Programming," class members have learned, is bad; "consciousness raising" is good. Yet many older women remain mothers and housewives and say they like it that way and that it is just as meaningful as going off to work every day.

And then there has always been abortion, which, since class members were eight, has been legal during the first three months of pregnancy. Even so, many individuals have mixed feelings about the morality of this procedure and its availability. Their grandparents may have told them they've never seen such intense anger propelling an issue since they themselves were children, when leaders of the temperance movement were railing about the evils of drink. Class members may even be aware, on some level, that the Supreme Court decision has meant a baby sibling they'll never have or an essential job that Mom can now keep.

* * * *

It wasn't just blacks and women and Indians who felt the system wasn't working and needed a major makeover. The American public was pervasively unhappy. Class members can't remember a popular president, unless you count Ronald Reagan, and even he was rather unpopular until just lately, as the economy has gotten better. Richard Nixon, the first president they would remember, was the embodiment of secrecy and suspicion, and he left office in ignominy. The next one, Gerald Ford, pardoned the previous one and, despite his athletic background, seemed doomed to suffer pratfalls both physical and verbal, along with assassination attempts. When they were eleven, he said in a widely televised debate with Jimmy Carter that the Soviet Union didn't dominate Eastern Europe. Even they knew better.

At first, President Carter seemed to be just what everyone wanted: moralistic and unpretentious, as he vowed never to lie to the public and always to be competent. His folksy southern demeanor seemed aligned with the emergence of the Sun Belt and of what one commentator called the "low WASP funk" of citizens band (CB) radios and newly popular country music. But his feckless proposals about energy independence—which he called "the Moral Equivalent of War"—were dubbed "MEOW" by one columnist. Every time a family member bought a Big Mac or a package of Instant Breakfast, it seemed that the price had gone up. Iranian radicals who had strongly opposed the overthrown Shah, a U.S. ally, captured our embassy personnel, and nothing this president tried to do about it came close to succeeding. The only good thing that came out of it was that new late-evening news show, *Nightline*, which their parents sometimes watched instead of Johnny Carson.

In another bummer, Americans didn't even participate in the 1980 Summer Olympics, held in Moscow, because the Soviets had invaded Afghanistan—something the Russians had told President Carter they would never do. Toward the end of his term he gave a downer speech about the American spirit, and while he didn't actually say that we were suffering from "malaise," everyone thought he did because that's what he had come to personify.

To be sure, the tall ships in New York Harbor had been impressive on July 4, 1976—two hundred years after the Declaration of Independence—but the birthday nation, having suffered the first of two major oil shocks thanks to the Organization of Petroleum Exporting Countries (OPEC), was energy dependent on endless gas lines and seemed anxious, timid, and sullen despite the parades and cherry pies. As if to reflect their feelings about the future, women were marrying later and having children later or not at all. The glut of babies that boomed after World War II has now ceased to be. Nonetheless, for members of the class of '83, who were eleven at the time of the Bicentennial, the red, white, and blue of that day might well have seemed like a hopeful light amid darker, more discouraging times.

If members of the class of 1983 feel they've been cheated a bit, they are not alone. Their grandparents had felt the same way about the thirties, but at least then there was the charisma of FDR, the cheer of the movies, and strong family ties. Now along with the bad economic times came rampant illegal drug use—coke is no longer only a soft drink—plus trivial fads (like Pet Rocks), endless gasoline lines, and restless minorities. In fact, it was not unusual for class members' grandparents to be the paradigm of tradition in their extended families. They may have hardly spoken to each other for years, but at least grandmother and grandfather were still married. Their own parents have always had almost a 50 percent chance of being divorced; and a family with a working father, a nonworking mother, and dependent children is now in the minority. The very acronyms of the 1970s—WIN, NOW, ERA, AIM, SLA, and OPEC—have all bespoken disappointment and failed expectations. Grandpa and Granny, now retired after cashing in their nest eggs from a more prosperous time after the war, seem much better off than class members' parents ever expect to be.

Distrust of government—fueled by a witches' brew of widespread suspicion and endless conspiracy theories about the Kennedy and King murders, Vietnam, and Watergate—has so pervaded the nation that some political leaders began wearing American flag pins in their lapels, as if to endorse the country's traditions and signal that it may have a bright future, after all.

* * * *

The previous decade had been more exciting, more idealistic, and more united. There was a discernible link between the Kennedys, Dr. King, Pope John XXIII, and the Beatles. They all inspired a reexamination of old assumptions about law, justice, nuclear testing, war, and peace—and the deeper meaning of rock. Members of the class of '83 have been the beneficiaries of that legacy. The priest has always stood facing the parishioners. Lively folk masses have become common. Ted Kennedy still offers handsome hope, in spite of some personal failings. "The dream shall never die," he proclaimed when they were high-school freshmen. But they will never grow up hearing the Beatles live and all together, for they have broken up irrevocably, and singer and songwriter John Lennon was gunned down when they were fifteen. While there was one big war going on, everyone was united in opposition, but now that it's over, the various protest movements have gone their own ways.

In the meantime the country remained divided between left and right. That had been true since the time they were born, as traditional patriots with traditional values began to balk at the idea of supporting the Viet Cong, taking off one's clothes in public, and giving Negroes—an increasingly outmoded term—special breaks. Even as class members were toddlers itching to go out and play, many of their fellow countrymen were itching to turn right and put an end to all this promiscuity and rioting, this losing an "unjust" war, and this new and scary talk about going beyond equal opportunity in matters of race in order to guarantee equal results. They thought they were getting a conservative in Nixon, but he disassembled very few of President Johnson's Great Society programs, never brought the country together, was forced from office—and *still* didn't win the damned war. In the absence of

a national conservative leader, many traditional citizens, especially below the Mason-Dixon line, turned to preachers, who
were founding universities, hosting daytime talk shows, and
even establishing theme parks for the vacationing faithful,
including a baptismal water slide.

It's always been a noisy and glittery time—with a din of
new voices and a kaleidoscope of new images. As the country
has become very young—a near majority, thanks to the baby
boomers, was under thirty when class members were born—the
audience for rock has aged. Popular culture, despite the glum
times, has continued to display a clever and jaunty ambience. In
the wake of the Beatles' implacably harmonious plea to give
peace a chance have come glam rock, heavy metal, punk, and
disco. Even mellow rock has found a place—all quite varied and
perplexing. David Bowie as Ziggy Stardust with his orange hair
and sparkling threads has become the new face of rock; he's
beautiful and bisexual but mostly just an outrageous performer— an expression of "let's see how far we can take this"
rather than a voice for a courageous new order. Meanwhile, hard
rockers have screamed and punk rockers have rasped out their
vile lyrics.

And then there was that throbbing disco dance music, a
strange blend of jazz and swing and blues—and synthesized
sound. When class members were about to enter middle school,
disco, via the famous Studio 54 in New York City, came to be
linked with the newly fashionable use of cocaine among the
wealthy and famous. Coke, so desired for its instant euphoria,
became a legally controlled and federally outlawed substance by
1970. To Studio 54, whether they scored coke or not, have come
megastar musicians, models, actors, and artists and the celebri-
ties whom one commentator dubbed "being well known for

being well known." Every night at the club a giant twinkling coke spoon would descend from the ceiling to great hilarity and applause.

But now disco, and all the dance clubs it inspired, has gone almost as soon as it came, as though offering a perverse tribute to the disposable frivolities of the era. Rock bands have been outdoing one another in the search for strange and disturbing names, from Led Zeppelin to the Sex Pistols and even a band called New Math. How long will they endure? Yet the rise of punk rock has been an inevitable trend, as young rock fans feel that more classic rock has become housebroken and packaged by large corporations. Rock has become far more diverse as its fans, amid a collection of performers who have apparently "sold out," search for the authentic.

Just as rock has diversified into an arguable confusion, so has more mainstream consumption. A country and western singer has asked if the good times were over for good and wondered plaintively why Chevy and Ford can't make cars "that last ten years like they should." More radical commentators have even suggested that these cars are made *not* to last so that Americans will have to buy new ones sooner, and that "planned obsolescence" is a bad joke played on American consumers. Regardless of the truth, even their grandparents now drive Datsuns and Toyotas and Volkswagens and wonder aloud whether the Germans and the Japanese didn't win the war after all. The tricky seatbelts in Volkswagen Beetles are called "Hitler's Revenge." Less stuff is manufactured here now, and as labor unions decline and more manufacturing occurs overseas in places such as China and Japan, class members have never known a United States that had a trade surplus with the rest of the world.

Frivolous fads seem to celebrate the pointlessness of a post-idealistic time. Elizabeth Taylor has lost weight in order to don hot pants in public. Fast-selling mood rings with their varying colors, depending upon the wearer's temperature, have always been seen as a way to communicate one's emotions. "Leisure suits" have always, by their name alone, been contradictory presentations of belted, boxy cloth in colors ranging from earth tones to poison green. Yet Dad has had two or three in polyester, hot as they may have been and cheap and vulgar as his parents thought they looked. Citizens Band radios have become popular not just with truckers but with average consumers in conservative places such as Indiana, where those from the town of Peru might take the outrageous "handle" "King of Peru." In a time of bewilderingly varied consumption and underlying pessimism, "Come on" and "Negatory, good buddy" have become part of the American CB vocabulary. For a while you could exchange pleasantries with strangers over the new short-wave radio in your car as a new definition of American unity. But by the time class members had turned fifteen, CBs had become just another vanishing trend.

It's always been okay, if you assume that the promising sixties are over and everything is just totally messed up, to retreat into the self. Jogging—and the tracksuits known as "jogging chic"—is really the thing to do now. If you can't control Nixon, Ford, Carter, stagflation, the oil shocks, or the Iranian hostage crisis, you can at least regulate your own body tone. No wonder Dad and Mom took up running, in what Grandpa, an ex-marine, might have called a double-time. Younger Americans got into Primal Screams, Hare Krishna, and Esalen. An unconventional uncle or aunt might have joined the Reverend Sun Myung Moon's Unification Church. And the members of this class have grown up with the reassurance that "I'm OK and you're OK." A best-selling pop psychology book has soothingly insisted on that.

When class members were too young to watch them, there were movies that would have exposed their parents or older siblings to the phoniness of a life based on "plastics," or the hypocrisies of middle-class liberals when faced with a mixed-race marriage in their own households, or the sexual freedom enjoyed by once-reviled robbers during the Depression. As class members have grown up to watch flicks of their own time, films have darkened, or morphed into blockbusters. The greatest film of their young lives so far, *The Godfather*, has managed to do both. A harrowing study of how even well-meaning power turns into brooding and punishing evil, the film has also afforded all the garish entertainment once brought by opera in the nineteenth century. This motion picture, along with *The Conversation* and *Chinatown*, has summoned the film noir of Hollywood's 1940s and blended it with all the distrust of power appropriate to an age when officials lied about everything from war to cover-ups, and even lied about not lying to us.

As members of the class of '83 have gotten old enough to go to more adult movies themselves, they've found films made for widespread appeal, from the "blaxploitation" films featuring the flamboyant and sexy Shaft, always victorious over hapless white villains, to the new summer blockbuster genre with great special effects such as *Jaws* and the *Star Wars* series. The closest that *Jaws* came to questioning power was its display of the buffoonish mayor who insisted the beaches stay open despite the shark attacks, even though the film itself kept many real sun worshipers out of the water the summer they were ten. The extended space opera *Star Wars* proved that the space program in which all Americans once took pride—it sent men to the moon when class members were just four—had become routine, despite the launching of Skylab, and required some significant high-tech upgrading. Therefore Luke will forever be vaporizing the Empire's Death Star. Meanwhile, the most horrifying film of the period, *The Exorcist*, has been another special-effects wonder and box office megasuccess, with shockingly profane language from a child who spewed oatmeal and pea soup—all designed to make millions. Its main impact on society has been to increase requests for exorcisms from parents who had exhausted other therapeutic options with difficult children.

The films are like jogging: a form of escape. If the nation has not been able to escape the revelations of Watergate and the loss of Vietnam, it can at least divert its gaze toward Bruce the Shark and Obi-Wan Kenobi. And if young filmmakers can't bust the Establishment, then they can at least bust previous attendance records. At the end of one such success, *The Towering Inferno*, about a new skyscraper that burns to the ground because of shoddy wiring by a corrupt contractor, the three main stars reflect upon the massive damage. One, the fire marshal, says the corruption will never cease. Another, the architect, says every building should be turned into manure and forgotten about. The last, the building's owner, says that he'll do everything he can to make sure it will never happen again, yet it seems likely that he will never be allowed to *build* anything again.

Such mordant banalities, at the end of a profitable blockbuster, have seemed typical of the era in which the class of '83 has come to maturity. Yet all of this stuff—from mood rings to megahits—has been done smartly. The denimed protests of the previous decade have been lucratively co-opted, so that now there are blue-jean leisure suits and even blue-jean Bible covers.

What could better express the absurdity of such an era than the Coneheads, an alien family that insists it is funny-looking only because it is from France? If Americans have lost their way, they have not lost their cleverness.

* * * *

As these young people begin to head off to college during this summer of 1983, their fellow Americans can point out that at least the seventies are over. President Reagan, who once served as spokesman for a company that insisted on "progress" as its "most important product," pledges new hope. Some things are clear so far. He doesn't share an earlier preoccupation with using government to achieve more equal blessings for all. He has all the pluck of the charming survivor, as evidenced by his seemingly facile but also moving recovery from an assassin's wound. He believes in an old-fashioned notion of the country, when taxes were low and personal responsibility and enterprise were high. He prefers even murderous regimes in Central America if they are able to keep Commie regimes at bay. Yet he seems to package those old verities in terms of a new sense of American adventure. For him, those who claim to be unable to achieve their goals because of race, class, or gender have simply not taken advantage of American opportunity.

In some ways Reagan seems a continuation of the previous decade. If that decade had its oxymoronic leisure suits, then the president has his oxymoronic "Laffer Curve," the theory that the way to collect more taxes is to lower them. At a time when the economy has baffled even the professionals, President Reagan speaks of a "supply-side economics" that his own vice president once called "voodoo economics." It seems too soon to determine whether the president is a return to a truer America or just his own, more traditional notion of the blockbuster seventies, with his own catchy phrases such as "Reaganomics," "the evil empire," and "peace through strength." Will these last longer than mood rings and moon shoes?

For a time he was unpopular because of continuing economic woes. Now there are signs of burgeoning recovery, led by the fact that 20 percent interest rates and national energy conservation have slowed the bad old 1970s inflation. Jogging seems to be more than a craze and may be improving the stamina of American millions. News has surfaced about other, happier acronyms, such as LISA (Local Integrated Software Architecture) and GUI (Graphical User Interface) that may somehow bring the controlled lightning of computers into the ordinary home. Maybe LISA and GUI will replace OPEC and SLA in American memory. All this seems promising as class members ready themselves for college, even as the witches' brew of baking soda, water, and cocaine, a cheap and accessible substance called "crack," may be moving drug use in an ominous new direction. Regardless, some members of the class of '83 can already "process" something into an Apple II computer and print it out on a dot-matrix printer, or jog to the rhythmic throbs of the Bee Gees on a Sony Walkman—disco is still good music for running—or spend a Susan B. Anthony dollar coin.

There are more women in the workforce than there have ever been before, and many more than there were when members of the class of 1983 were born. This development appears to be a source of future economic vigor—it's something our rivals the Japanese have not done—after the country has gone through such a tough time. Words like "Ms." and "gay" have become increasingly accepted without resentment or embarrassment. The good news is that Mom is working and makes her daughters see that they, too, can have a career once they finish college in 1987. The bad news is that Mom and Dad have split up, but they both seem happier.

Meanwhile, there are new films for class members to see before they head off to college. One, *The King of Comedy*, is a dark study of a man who will do almost anything to get on national television, however fleeting and asinine his moment in the spotlight may be. Another, *The Right Stuff*, celebrates the enduring astronautical heroism of a not-so-long-ago decade. It is hard to tell which film, if either, will better represent America's—and the class of 1983's—future. Will it be one of unremitting self-involvement, of brave new sacrifice, or neither?

Michelangelo Has Always Been a
Turtle

Members of this class were born in 1978 and graduated from high school in 1996; they would become the millennial college class of 2000.

Class members include Clay Aiken (born Clay Grissom), second-place winner in the 2003 season of *American Idol*; basketball star Kobe Bryant; and Katie Holmes, actor and wife of Tom Cruise.

Former vice president Hubert Humphrey, artist Norman Rockwell, Morris the Cat, and American-born Israeli prime minister Golda Meir have always been dead.

Mindset List

1. There have always been "57 channels and nothin' on."

2. Jerry Falwell has always been the unofficial spiritual guru of the Grand Old Party.

3. Americans have always been spelling "trouble" M-I-D-E-A-S-T.

4. Their grandparents have now outlived the Soviet Union.

5. Deregulation has always been mainstream.

6. On Wall Street, tobacco and cookies go together nicely, thank you.

7. They have secretly agreed with Bart Simpson when he wished he could be a grown-up so he, too, could break the rules.

8. The best way to rob a bank has been to own one.

9. American League pitchers have never gotten their at-bats, while free agency has meant that players have always been able to take their swings at the negotiating table.

10. Rock music and TV have always cohabited.

11. McDonald's has always been counting burgers in the billions.

12. ABC has always seen the news 20/20.

13. AM radio has always been right.

14. Their baseball bats have always gone "ping."

15. Their second-grade teacher had to comfort them moments after the *Challenger* blew up.

16. Bill Gates has always been "in the chips"—but they've probably never used this expression.

17. Used spacecraft have always been as common as used cars.

18. Peking has always been Beijing.

19. Discussing condoms in mixed company has become less and less embarrassing.

20. They have always observed Martin Luther King Jr. Day in their schools, and always been advised to Just Say No.

21. There have always been TV dramas about rich folks and their trashy behavior.

22. Michelangelo, Donatello, Raphael, and Leonardo have always been turtles.

23. Until they were teens, they could never officially get into a raunchy or violent movie without their parents.

24. They've always thought of Dustin Hoffman as a sensitive guy who plays cross-dressing or autistic men.

25. A woman's image has always been circulating on a coin.

26. Exercise has always been hot.

27. They'll probably take their Cabbage Patch Kids adoption papers to a goofy college party.

28. Game Boys have made many a cross-country auto trip with their parents more tolerable.

29. MBA has always meant "Making it Big in America."

30. They've grown up to see the Chinese cracking down, and the Russians standing down, in the same year.

31. A black woman has frequently been found on the upper right corner of a first-class mail

envelope; civil rights leaders have always been celebrated on stamps.

32. They've sung and danced to "I Heard It through the Grapevine" along with a bunch of Claymation raisins.

33. Networking has always been better than working.

34. They always had to sit in car seats when they were little and wear bike helmets as they got older.

35. People have always been willing to talk about intimate things to millions of people in real time on television.

36. The most important philosophers in their lives have been Miss Piggy, Mr. Rogers, Dr. Huxtable, and Yoda.

37. With images of mass suicide in Jonestown still on her mind, Mom has always felt a bit squeamish about urging the kids to drink their Kool-Aid.

38. After seeing *Fatal Attraction*, their parents might have reassessed their relationship.

39. They've always been able to watch wars and riots in real time.

40. Analog technology is as quaint to them as horse-drawn carriages were to their grandparents.

41. In middle school and high school it's been increasingly okay not to have sex.

42. There have always been Elvis impersonators, but no Elvis.

43. Switching religions once or twice has always been common in the United States.

44. They have become the most sought-after buyers of media products in the land.

45. It's been hard to know which was more entertaining—the actual scandal or the made-for-TV movie ripped from the headlines.

46. While they worried about driving the family car, Harry and Louise worried about keeping the family doctor.

47. In vitro fertilization (IVF) has never been a crime against nature.

48. They've attended schools rife with strife about testing, vouchers, and book banning.

49. Mom and Pop businesses and local charge accounts have almost disappeared from Main Street.

50. Unlike the Artist Formerly Known as Prince, computers have become less mysterious with every passing year.

* * * *

During the nineties, as members of this class were moving toward high school, there was a popular T-shirt proclamation that '90s MUSIC LIVES. These sartorial declarations have been abroad in the land since the 1960s, and here it certainly seems okay to wax prematurely nostalgic for grunge and ripped jeans and combat boots and Kurt Cobain, or for alternative rock and Sarah McLachlan and Lilith Fair and all-female rock groups. It's quite all right to note that the venerable band Smashing Pumpkins has never had anything to do with smashing pumpkins. And after all, it was in 1995, the year before class members graduated from high school, that Cleveland got one of its best ideas and established the Rock and Roll Hall of Fame on the anything-but-rocking shores of Lake Erie.

Still, this humble and low-tech pronouncement seems to pale as a reminder of a decade that changed our everyday vocabulary—"The server's down. "See you online."—and our rules of writing— lowercase for everything including your proper name and smiley sign-offs. The class of 1996 may have been the first one to grow up believing that anything technical is possible, that Arthur C. Clarke was correct when he said that there is no real difference between magic and high technology, and that if they can read text by scrolling it up and down on a screen, then they may someday read text on a cellular phone or on a portable book screen carried in their Trapper Keepers. Someday they won't need to carry books at all. They've been the first generation to grow up thinking that films didn't necessarily have to have much human drama if they had the special effects produced by that mix of magic and high technology. They go without media and information only when asleep—and one day they'll even figure out how to provide the stuff for their nightly dreams, too! The truly great music of the '90s was not pop, but the barely audible clicking of millions of computer keyboards in millions of homes ☺.

* * * *

The high school class of 1996, which will form the nucleus of the much celebrated and overcharged college class of 2000, was in the second or third grade when their teachers switched on the TV so that they could watch the *Challenger* spacecraft take off with a teacher on board who had planned, within a few days, to conduct classes via satellite hookup from outer space. If, however, teachers on Earth forgot to turn on the TV, they were relieved, for otherwise they would have had to comfort children shaken by the subsequent explosion, which was, for most of them, the first truly traumatic experience of their lives. By then "used" space vehicles were becoming as common as used cars; they could be sent into space over and over again and then returned to Earth. This one didn't make it. Some days later President Ronald Reagan comforted the nation by asserting that the seven dead astronauts, who included not only a female teacher but also an African American male physicist, had slipped "the surly bonds of earth to touch the face of God."

Members of the class of '96 have grown up with a different take on space-age technology—not that it sometimes requires consolation from the president but that it is a cosmic drama, an infinitely amusing game, and a chance to love those very different from themselves. They've matured by navigating the Nintendo Game Boy's never-ending mazes, harnessing the Force against the predatory Empire, and saving the lives of cute but homely little aliens by bicycling them to safety past the moon. Sometimes their toys have been low-tech, as with the Cabbage Patch dolls complete with adoption papers, and leathery but snuggly little extraterrestrials, but generally it's been high-tech, as with the Teddy Ruxpin bear, who told them neat stories, or the alternative-reality cartoon figures such as the Care Bears from the land of Care-a-lot or Leonardo and Raphael, the Teenage Mutant Ninja Turtles, or the Claymation raisins who did their own version of Motown.

They are the second generation of latchkey kids, either with both parents working or just a single parent under the family roof. Clay Grissom, a member of the class who is also a popular singer in the Raleigh, North Carolina, area, may soon change his last name from that of his estranged father to Aiken, the surname of his grandparents. But exceptions to the rule of family fission have been plentiful, too, and they've included Katie Holmes, born in Toledo to a homemaker mother and a lawyer father. A wholesome and brilliant girl, and a devout Catholic, she scored 1300 out of 1610 on her SATs and was accepted at Columbia University, where she attended a summer session before shifting her sights to Hollywood. At eighteen she landed a supporting role in the independent film *The Ice Storm*. Her wholesomeness has been a good choice, for her generation has grown up with cautionary tales relating to AIDS and other sexually transmitted diseases. Unlike the previous generation, they learned about these realities before they became sexually mature, and they've rarely seen free sex as a birthright. In fact, they seemed increasingly comfortable with the idea of abstinence.

As they approached their teens, they witnessed a rapidly changing world order with images of a lone Chinese student in a standoff against a column of enormous Chinese tanks, the new Soviet leader standing on another tank in Moscow in order to defy the old Communist generals, and the hammering down of the real and symbolic Berlin Wall. They've learned to play soccer in their neighborhood leagues, often strictly monitored by their organization-conscious parents, who also put bike helmets on them and have always been really, really concerned about their safety and success, denying them a child's God-given right to lick the bowl and the beaters because the cookie dough contained raw eggs. Their America has been one in which sales of stretch limos have skyrocketed, restless citizens have frequently changed religions, and a majority of people have apparently always believed in angels. It's been a time of rampant consumerism, but also of growing religious and spiritual interest. Americans have shopped for churches just as they have shopped in the big-box stores that have continued to drive out the familiar family-owned shops that had been there for generations.

* * * *

This generation of Americans was born one year too late for membership in what an author in 1991 called Generation X. That, it seems, is more than just a matter of the calendar, for this generation has always seemed different from their immediate forebears. When Gen Y was born in 1978, the country was in trouble, with a seemingly clueless president, rampant inflation and sluggish growth, and vulnerability to the whims of oil lords in the Mideast. By the time they were just starting to walk and talk, things got worse. There was a second "oil shock," prompted by hatred of Americans especially in places such as Iran, and the humiliation of American hostages being held in Tehran for what seemed to be an endless period of powerlessness, ticked off daily on the evening news. By the time they came to political and social awareness of any sort, everything seemed to have gotten better. They've rarely known presidents who were overwhelmed by the job. Unlike their acerbic, cynical predecessors—the Gen Xers who tried to master the laugh of the obnoxious and lazy Beavis and Butt-Head and grew up as the first latchkey-kid generation and grooved on outrageous characters like Dennis Rodman—they've lived in a far more optimistic time. From the booming morning-glory optimism of Ronald Reagan to the digital revolution and subsequent economic boom that it ushered in, they've been part of an America with a greater spring in its step, even as an undercurrent of menacing organized violence and troubling economic adjustment has marred its otherwise happy dawns.

For this class certain social experiences have always been normal, and most of them trace back to the technological revolution through which they've lived. In the memorable words of Bruce Springsteen, there have always been "57 channels and nothin' on." He exaggerated, of course, for this generation has grown up with an array of choices, thanks to the growth of something else: cable TV, including a channel on which the music video—once a cheap and throwaway vehicle for publicizing a rock music performer or album—has become a new art form. Veejays have now replaced deejays. What was once confined to radio—rock—has, in their experience, always been on television. The prudent and cautious fare offered by the Big Three networks has always had competition from the far more daring menu of cable. Through cable they've had access to raunchy music videos, talk shows in which anything and everything has been discussed (seemingly without embarrassment), networks devoted entirely to old movies and TV shows long past their initial syndication, and even their own cartoon network (with shows that had to be rated for age-propriety). Cable has given them choices and entrée to realms never found on NBC, CBS, and ABC. And as they have gotten into their teens, a new and edgier network, Fox, has joined the fray. The whole viewing experience has become rather like those network shows, such as *Dallas* and *Falcon Crest*, about rich people behaving badly: trashy, yes, but also glitzy and enthralling.

* * * *

The same has been true for that other great technology—this one far more revolutionary—with which the class of 1996 has grown up, and it too, like cable, has involved a transparent screen. When they were born, there were hardly any personal computers, and the first ones were primitive, without a screen— or, as this generation has learned to call it, a "monitor"—and no easy way to manipulate the instructions to the machines with what they would soon enough call a "mouse." But by the time they were getting ready to enter middle school, they could easily go to their parents and say that if they don't get an Apple with its word-processing and floppy disks, they will fall behind in school. Before long the parents, too, joined the program and began to order flowers and rent cars without having to make a telephone call. Indeed, by the time they got to high school, a new feature of computerized power greeted all of them happily: the interconnected network, via special phone lines, appropriately called the Internet. In time they would be able to send messages around the globe and visit commercial, political, and educational "websites," in addition to those of almost every news outlet, print and otherwise. Knowing the difference between "dot-com" and "dot-net" has become as important as knowing the distinction between peanut butter and bread. If they have had a summer abroad in Sweden and met some kids over there, they could now "talk" to them in real time. Family members began to fight over who would get the computer next.

Monitors became colorized. Macintosh and IBM divided the world between them. By the time class members were in high school, it was evident that the new technology meant that problems could be analyzed, collaboration could be sharpened, and information could be tracked and stored in a measure undreamt of just fifteen years earlier. American productivity and labor could be increased without the side effect of inflation. Tech stocks became as hot as the Sex Pistols used to be. The nineties seem to roar, albeit in the privacy of homes quietly driving on the information superhighway, as even the eighties had not.

If the class of 1918 had a revolutionary familiarity with the words "ignition" and "spark plugs," this generation has acquired a similar revolutionary understanding of "hardware" and "software." All of this has been courtesy of something called a "silicon chip," as tiny as the tip of one's finger and yet capable of holding myriad amounts of electronic connections in quantities that could be counted precisely thanks to embedded digital instructions based on infinite combinations of zero and one. It was not long after this generation was born that nondigital, or analog, technology started to become as quaint as the horse and carriage. Radios and watches no longer operated on the inexact personally adjusted "dial" principle—although you could still buy them that way—but were premised instead on exact read-outs of stations and times. Above all, though, there was tele-phone and radio reception, which took voices from far away and transformed them into precise digital signals for much more crystalline reception. Bill Gates, who was emperor of software programs, and Steve Jobs, who was king of hardware design and marketing, have become both magnificently wealthy and inter-nationally famous. They both went digital in a pivotal way, and now both are in the chips, both the monetary and the silicon species.

Now this generation's elders are trying to figure out what this new technology means. Does it portend a succession of generations who would rather "process" conversations online than have them face-to-face? Will reading "on-screen" mean the end of books? Will the new spell-checkers mean the end of "*i* before *e* except after *c*"? Will learning become more and more self-directed and lonely? Above all, what does all of this suggest about parents being able to control their kids' access to informa-tion? Two generations ago, stuck with the Big Three networks, kids might have watched *The Andy Griffith Show* with their par-ents and laughed at the cornpone human foibles of Barney and

Gomer right along with their elders. But now there is cable and now there are computers. And there are second and maybe even third TVs in the house, and soon enough Junior and Peg will have their own computers, too. Will this new generation come to inhabit a separate universe all their own? And what will that universe be like? It's something that even phlegmatic Ronald Reagan might be tempted to worry about.

If their parents were able to bring themselves to watch and listen to MTV, they would have seen and heard what sorts of things *were* in that universe apart. These parents have always had an ear for rock, for, after all, theirs was the first generation of parents to have gotten older with the stuff—unlike their own parents, whose idea of a musical good time was still Lawrence Welk and what was left of the Hotsy Totsy Boys. Taste in rock, though, is honed over time, and for the parents it's been sentimentally a matter of the Beatles and Pink Floyd and the Stones and maybe, for the older parents, a little Elvis and Carl Perkins and Lloyd Price and Buddy Holly thrown in, too. Their parents were into Michael Jackson and Lionel Richie's song "We Are the World," composed as a fund-raiser for African nations and performed by a star-studded chorus on international television. What would these parents have thought had they dropped in on music videos featuring Michael Jackson's androgynous Fred Astaire–like moves and falsetto tones; or Madonna's never-look-the-same-way-twice, garish materialism? What about the punks with an earring for every orifice and a spike for every follicle of hair, or the rappers with their street beat and streetwise lyrics? At least one boomer, Tipper Gore, the wife of a U.S. senator and eventual vice president, testified to Congress that some of these lyrics were outrageously suggestive and evil. And Gore was a Democrat, which was supposed to be, or so their enemies always said, the party of permissiveness and pot.

* * * *

Unlike the previous generation, which witnessed the implosion of the Democratic Party into a factional group seemingly devoted to the interests of society's underdogs, or of everyone but the middle class, this generation has seen the rise of the Republicans as the dominant American political party. Whether or not class members were ever fully aware of Ronald Reagan when they were kids, he has been the preeminent political figure of their young lives. Ever optimistic and folksy and yet paradoxically magisterial, too, he has presided over an America of good economic times, innovative technology, entrepreneurial creativity, predatory finance, and distrust of expansive government. He has watched the profound relocations of power and money from the northern part of the country, with its declining unions and heavy manufacturing, to the southern, with its low taxes, high tech, and inviting climate. The World According to Reagan has been one of foreign policy victories—from tiny Grenada to the mammoth deals with the Soviets to destroy nuclear weapons—and of apparent clueless confusion about what his staff was doing with hostages and weapons and Nicaragua; and of ever-burgeoning tax cuts and government deficits; and of Flint, Michigan, and other Rust Belt cities as sites of astonishing shrinkage. With Reagan, Teflon has come in handy for both skillets and political figures. When asked if he worried about the deficit, he said, why, no, because "it's big enough to take care of itself." With such an affable quip, why should anyone else worry?

If Reagan's policies toward the poor seemed heartless—as government money was pulled from school lunch programs, Republican bureaucrats counted ketchup as a vegetable in order to save money—his aides always said that he was a kind man who would personally give you the shirt off his back. Besides, there was a new morality in town—not of liberal compassion but of conservative concerns about abortion, pornography, and homosexuality. The Reverend Jerry Falwell has become the spiritual guru of the Republicans. Yet—in another paradox—while President Reagan always seemed to stand with Falwell and his followers, he has also presided over an America with increasingly audacious media content. Like a president he has long admired, Calvin Coolidge, Reagan has seemed something of a Puritan in Babylon, for like Coolidge, he has been president during a time both profligate and moralistic. But Reagan has always had a lot more show-biz moxie than the taciturn Cal could have ever even conceived. Coolidge was a man of one craggy face, Reagan of many sunny ones. He made conservatism seem not hidebound but forward-looking. If there has been a contradiction between the economic liberty and the stringent morality championed by Reagan, the president never bothered to acknowledge it. He has seemingly been too busy not fretting about anything in an America that, by his serene lights, can *do* anything.

Under Reagan the America of the class of 1996's childhood has embraced a new conservative can-do spirit and new conservative populism. It has been a heady time for a right-wing movement that seemed dead only twenty years earlier, with the dramatic defeat of Senator Barry Goldwater in the 1964 election. It's not clear, however, that class members themselves were affected much by what thrilled their elders, for in school they were learning about the civil rights heroics of the past, with reverence for the achievements of Martin Luther King Jr. and the annual holiday they have had since they were eight, and about the need to respect at all times those who are categorically different from the majority. U.S. postage stamps have celebrated Harriet Tubman and other African American leaders. The diversity discussion has been a perfect way to keep the kids in line, so under the nose of the Reagan Revolution has been a quiet campaign for tolerance that may result in a much more liberal future generation. This generation is also a polite one. They know Dustin Hoffman, for instance, not as the impish rebel against the meaninglessness of "plastics," as their parents did, but as a versatile performer who can play everything from cross-dressing actors to autistic men—characters who are, once again, categorically different from the mainstream.

* * * *

Looking back on this generation's lifetime from the perspective of their eighteenth year, one might speculate that just as their parents grew up in an America hungering for more cultural freedom, they themselves grew up hungering for more economic freedom. Thus both political parties sponsored a relaxation of government regulation of businesses and what they could or couldn't do. This deregulation has had a number of implications, but probably none more important than those for high finance. On Wall Street for a while there were suddenly more "raiders" than on the Oakland football team. They have engaged in "hostile takeovers" or "leveraged buyouts," to use the lingo of the time, not in order to make companies but in order, as one commentator has put it, to *unmake* them. The formula has been simple to describe but hard to carry out. If you're a raider, you find the financing to take over a company—even if it consists of high-yield but high-risk "junk bonds"—and you buy up most of the company's stock. Eventually you'll control the company; it's yours. You take it over, downsize it by firing lots of its workers, and then sell it for a huge profit not long after. It's always been a new ethic, not of manufacturing but of de-manufacturing, not of working but of networking. And if all this came across as unseemly to the American public, you could always have a flashy merger, as one major tobacco company did with a major food company—Camels, accompanied by Oreos, seem less malevolent.

Among the many enterprises deregulated were savings and loan companies. Once stodgy hometown lenders to individual customers for cars and homes, they have been permitted to get into high finance and engage in all sorts of risky business. The Feds also guaranteed them against losses to their customers. And losses they have certainly sustained, as their investments—as adventuresome as Indiana Jones's but without the happy outcome—came crashing down. Somebody quipped that the best way to rob a bank is to own one, and this has particularly applied to the piratical buccaneers who owned S&Ls. By the time class members were starting their senior year in high school, the process of tidying up after the S&Ls—and after the Exxon oil tanker *Valdez*—has gone on and on and on, with more and more billions required from taxpayers. None of these avaricious businessmen resembled compassionate old George Bailey with his wonderful life of fifty years earlier, and many Americans have agreed that life would have been much more wonderful fifty years later without such greedy buccaneers of the American enterprise system.

Although President Reagan seemed not to worry, there was plenty to worry about. Along with the newfound liberty came not just financial chicanery but also an increasing "my way or the highway" mentality imposed at the end of a gun barrel or with a stick of dynamite. Members of the class of '96 have found themselves in a land of secretive militias convinced that both the federal government and international businessmen were planning to put them in concentration camps; and in a country of religious fanatics quite prepared to shoot agents of the government's Alcohol, Tobacco, and Firearms enforcement bureau; and in a nation of loners so angry at the federal government that they would blow up a federal building in Oklahoma even if it housed a daycare center. Meanwhile, rules were changed to eliminate the requirement that radio stations give equal time to all points of view, and this has led to the rise of conservative AM radio, where thousands of Americans could phone in and express "ditto" disgust with the very idea of government rules through laws or transfer of wealth through taxes.

For all of the ways the members of the class of 1996 have lived in a contented America, replete with generally prosperous times and innovative technology and the end of the Cold War—their grandparents have now outlived the Soviet Union—many Americans have *not* been contented. Among them have been gun groups in Idaho and laid-off blue-collar workers in Michigan and Indiana. Even as strutting Madonna has been flaunting the virtues of material success, and even as Jim and Tammy Faye Baker have been insisting that if Christ were alive today he, too, would buy luxurious refrigerators, there has been a darker side to the go-go eighties and nineties. It has been experienced by both those who feel there isn't enough political liberty and those who *know* there isn't enough economic security.

* * * *

After all the dodgy practices of Wall Street and the S&Ls when class members were children, they were greeted in their teens by a renewed emphasis on personal responsibility, along with consumer-driven excess, innovative media mixes, and new forms of poverty. The new levels of responsibility were largely placed upon the poor, who saw their welfare benefits made much more conditional upon getting and keeping a job, and onto deadbeat dads, who were disgraced by publicity about their trifling ways and had their bank accounts garnished until they ponied up. Conservatives, and even some liberals, applauded these new rules, yet the new theme of personal responsibility seemed contradicted by other aspects of the culture, including made-for-television movies rushed into video almost as soon as the scandal on which they were based was over, and sometimes even beforehand. The unseemly stories of Amy Fisher's shooting her older lover's wife or the Menendez brothers' offing their parents or David Koresh's fanatical standoff in Waco, Texas, against the Feds soon came to a major television network, just a quick click away on the remote.

Indeed, an epoch that has stressed personal responsibility has also been one of new excess, as some former radical yippies from the 1960s have enjoyed a great vowel shift. Now termed *yu*ppies, these Young Urban Professionals both work and network assiduously, the better to pay the steep bills for their BMWs, their capacious Jacuzzis, and their costly Levi's jeans, with the red label quite conspicuous, of course. They seem primed to be both countercultural and upper-middle-class at the same time. It is not the yuppies, however, but members of the class of 1996, and others about their age, who have become the single most sought-after consumers of media products in the land. This began with Nintendo, but now, as they are teens, it has expanded to include Air Jordans and the Walkman and the Sega Genesis. They have roamed the increasingly popular big-box stores in an ongoing quest for new and necessary forms of entertainment.

Indeed, the class of 1996 has matured in what is now a whole new universe of media for everyone, where traditional categories have been irrevocably revised. Thus basketball stars are also fashion models, information and news have become profitable entertainment, Saturday morning adventure serials from the fifties have become full-length blockbuster films, and the smart-alecky cats and bunnies of cartoons past have become the preciously perverse little kids of Fox cartoons. What President George H. W. Bush called "the teenybopper network" (MTV) has become a political interview channel where Bill Clinton could hang out his clean underwear. Media even goes jogging now, thanks to the up-close and personal Walkman, and to exercise videos with fetching but never sweating Jane Fonda. Perhaps people jog a little more because they feel guilty about the indolence allowed by the TV remote. It seems a nice problem to have. Even nonmedia products have entered category gaps. Shampoo has fruit in it; water now comes in designer bottles.

Meanwhile, this era—of new responsibility and excess and relentless media creativity—has also been a time of poverty, both old and new. The new has become a familiar sight on the nation's city streets. The homeless reside obscurely in remote urban corners, perhaps sleeping it off behind their thick coats and knitted hats and keeping all their possessions in a rolling wire basket—or perhaps, during the day, squeegeeing car windshields at intersections. They might loom up suddenly in the darkness as class members and their parents are on their way to a sushi restaurant, and then kids from eight to eighteen would suddenly glimpse the dingy basement into which adults could fall. The growing multitudes of homeless people have arrived courtesy of bad habits, economic dislocation, and the recent trend of mental institutions being forced to let them go.

There were the ongoing challenges faced by African Americans, who continued to lead the nation in premature deaths, single motherhood, prison population, and death by homicide. A delightful exception was the classmate Kobe Bryant—his first name came from an item on a Japanese restaurant menu—whose father was a basketball star in the Philadelphia area and even in Italy. Young Kobe, who began to play the sport at three and has broken every Philadelphia high school basketball record, was destined to be the first guard drafted by the National Basketball Association out of high school.

* * * *

As the class of 1996 has lived through an age of great novelty in media and consumption and, alas, even poverty, the major historical developments of their childhood years have involved the end of the Cold War and the liberation of Eastern Europe. Their teen years have also witnessed a technological revolution that has reached far beyond information and entertainment. It has also extended and saved lives.

It turns out there is no cure for cancer—it will not be eradicated with a single shot as polio was for their parents—but there are effective new treatments for many different types of cancer, and the treatments trace and manage the diverse quirks of diverse tumors. The opportunity for women struggling to become pregnant has increased exponentially with embryo implants. Indeed, though it is unlikely, members of the class of 1996 may well have had younger siblings who originated in test tubes.

POEMS has had nothing to do with rhyme or verse but everything to do with Duke University's Post Operative Expert Medical System, an immense database with all sorts of information that physicians from all backgrounds and specialties can access—through the computer, of course—on how to treat their patients all over the planet. Our destiny, it turns out, is in our genes as much as in anything else. When class members were becoming teens, it was announced that scientists would eventually track every single human gene, with the prospect of altering or implanting genes in order to cure or prevent serious maladies.

If the personal computer has raised questions about what sorts of social skills the first computerized generation would have, genetic research has stimulated discussion about whether people should be told in advance that they have potentially lethal genes and whether they would be able to get insurance to cover them for anything. With progress comes perplexity, an old story, but the class of 1996 has clearly entered a brave new world.

* * * *

Their de facto favorite philosophers, as they have moved from childhood to high school commencement, have been Miss Piggy, Mr. Rogers, Dr. Heathcliff Huxtable, and Yoda. From Miss Piggy they have learned to keep going strong in spite of, and even because of, obvious foibles. Their parents, when the kids were toddlers, even got from her all sorts of wonderfully wacky book advice about beauty, diet, travel, and money. It was Miss Piggy, needy and vulnerable and overcompensating, who said that since an artichoke weighs more than a pastry, eat the pastry. And it was she who has shown the kids watching *The Muppet Show* that it was perfectly okay to be needy and inse cure but to keep trying to get what you need, even if it's only Kermit. Mr. Rogers has reassured them that their parents' divorce wasn't really their fault at all, that being scared and hurt is a natural part of life, and that a balance between the real-life neighborhood and a make-believe world is healthy. Dr. Huxtable showed them that humor and suffering go beautifully together, that African Americans can be upper middle class and successful and professional, and that dyslexia and teen pregnancies are facts of American life. And then there has always been Yoda, who has taught them to take the cosmic view, train hard, resist impulsiveness, and become one with some Force or other.

For all the ways in which the class of 1996 has been overexposed to media, and despite Marshall McLuhan's warning that it's the medium and not the message that counts, class members have gotten some pretty good advice. As they are about to enter college, America seems more awash in peace and prosperity than at any time since the 1920s. Will bad economic times come again sooner than anyone might think? If so, then the world will see how faithfully the class of 1996 has absorbed the plucky counsel of their famous media philosophers.

They've Never Dialed a Telephone

Members of this class were born in 1991 and will graduate from high school in 2009. They will finish college in 2013.

Members of this class include actors Jamie Lynn Spears and Daniel Curtis Lee, and composer Jay Greenberg.

Dr. Seuss, comedian and philanthropist Danny Thomas, choreographer Martha Graham, jazz legend Miles Davis, and Pan American Airways have always been dead.

Mindset List

1. The Abominable Snowman of Pasadena has always given them Goosebumps.

2. With caller ID they've always known who's waiting on the line.

3. They've always wished Arnold Schwarzenegger really could have been their kindergarten teacher.

4. Beethoven has always been more than just a composer.

5. Before the boys cleared four feet in height, they wanted to be like Mike.

6. Unless they live near Waco or Oklahoma City, events in those communities are ancient history.

7. Before they were teens, they were already texting "lol & paw 2 thr frnds."

8. They identify with websites more than with states or religions.

9. They're the first generation in half a century to ask legitimately, "What Berlin Wall?"

10. Few of them have ever "written" a letter.

11. They can't figure out why anyone would bother to print out a whole set of encyclopedias.

12. They've never actually "dialed" a telephone.

13. Fax machines have always been soooo eighties.

14. TVs have always been flat.

15. One of them might win a Guinness World Record for multitasking.

16. They get most of their news from Comedy Central and *The Onion*.

17. They have met customer service, and it is they.

18. Courtesy of their iPhones or BlackBerries, they can walk and surf at the same time.

19. They've stayed up late with the Masturbating Bear and Conando.

20. They aren't sure why their college dorm room comes with a telephone wired to the wall.

21. They've grown up with "friend" as an active verb.

22. They think of Britney Spears as a "classic" rock singer.

23. Chairmen have always been "chairpersons" or "chairs," and actresses have always been "actors."

24. They just hate it when one of their friends is "emo."

25. The girls started out wanting to be like Barbie but later switched to Buffy.

26. Their parents have always worried about the R-rated humor they were picking up from Ren and Stimpy and Beavis and Butt-Head.

27. They never got carbon-paper ink stains on their hands from a credit card receipt.

28. They may have rolled their eyes in resigned agreement when their parents were compared to helicopters—but they still appreciate the ride.

29. Memory has always been doubling.

30. They studied hard in middle school with dreams of someday being admitted to Hogwarts.

31. They've always had strong emotions about freeing and saving whales.

32. Tattoos have never been déclassé.

33. Fergie has always been a singer, not a princess.

34. Within the first couple of weeks of fourth grade, their parents picked them up early from school to assure them they were safe despite the repeated TV images of planes crashing into buildings.

35. Swiping has always referred to how you buy something, not how you steal it.

36. One of their favorite YouTube videos has been a demonstration of the new "iRack," an unstable product on the verge of collapse with no exit strategy.

37. They've never cranked up a car window or used a card catalogue at the library, also known as the media center.

38. South Africa has never been legally segregated.

39. Nicaragua and El Salvador have always been calm, and have seldom been in the news.

40. Some of their friends might be disabled, but never handicapped.

41. They have grown up being tickled by Elmo.

42. They've always been able to vacation with their folks at Universal Studios Florida.

43. Antiviruses have been as important to them as antibiotics were to their grandparents.

44. The Kennedy tragedy was a plane crash off the coast of New England.

45. For all they know, Desert Storm is the name of a rock band.

46. Magic Johnson has always been HIV positive and has never developed AIDS.

47. While their parents may have been wishing for the Waltons, the kids were happily secure with the Simpsons.

48. They'll never be able to fly OnePass on Eastern.

49. No matter how desperately ill their grandparents may become, they will never be able to go to Dr. Jack Kevorkian for ultimate assistance.

50. They have gladly watched as their communications needs were compressed into the ever-tighter confines of a computer.

* * * *

Dr. Perri Klass is a pediatrician and a writer who promotes the idea that when kids see doctors, part of the "wellness" process is improving their literacy. Thus she urges doctors to spend some time reading to kids even as they spend time diagnosing them. This practice might seem anachronistic, for being read to would be extremely low-tech for a generation so immersed in new technology. Indeed, it is the first generation that is completely post–Cold War and supercomputerized. Although they have also grown up with low-tech Barney, that irresistible purple dinosaur, and although they have spent their hours being delightfully frightened by the latest Goosebumps book, one most often thinks of them perched in front of a PC or a Play Station or texting surreptitious messages "2 1 n other." Thus, reading to kids, as Dr. Klass recommends, seems more like something out of the 1940s or '50s.

But there is something quintessentially 1990s about her doing so as a doctor in her office. Indeed, this is what so much of the nineties and the first decade of the twenty-first century have been about: the transformation of decorum in social spaces. It was once considered quite mad to appear to talk to oneself loudly in public, but with the profusion of mobile phones the practice has come to be seen as normal. The only madness might rest in the fact that the speakers are so absorbed with conducting business on their Sprints or Motorolas that they can't sit calmly and watch people. Once upon a time, if a man held a hand to his ear, we would assume he was scratching it or cupping it or trying to staunch bleeding. But now it's only his razor-thin, handheld iPhone up there. Now bus drivers have to admonish passengers not to intrude upon the public space of fellow travelers with cell conversations. It would once have seemed annoying if a TV screen carried so much colorful lettering that one could barely follow the main picture. But such clutter is now common, and if one can't follow the news interview while also getting the crawling stock report, sports scores, and headlines at the same time, then one is obviously a geezer. Young people can do homework while listening to music, "chatting," and "surfing" all at once.

So why should it be unusual to think that a doctor can read and heal at once? And Dr. Klass isn't the only one; she has convinced many of her fellow physicians to do precisely the same—very, very nineties! The kids like it, too.

* * * *

Members of the high school class of 2009 dozed in safely designed cribs surrounded by a post–Cold War world, a world that was more serene than not. They were but gleams in their parents' eyes when the Berlin Wall came down. Before they were born, Belarus, Moldova, Ukraine, Uzbekistan, Armenia, Latvia, Georgia, Lithuania, and Estonia had spun out of the Soviet orbit. Since then, some of these countries have done better than others, but all are independent. Therefore the class of 2009 has been the first generation in nearly fifty years never to have fretted over the nuclear balance of power between their own country and the Soviet Union. Phrases such as "pushing the red button," "the black box," and "using the Red Telephone" have never worried them. They enjoyed a largely optimistic trajectory until their senior year in high school, when their country and their world narrowly missed another gargantuan economic depression.

They haven't been anxious over the Cold War, but that doesn't mean they haven't been scared. They grew up reading the monstrously frightening situations of the Goosebumps series, and R. L. Stine introduced them to the Abominable Snowman of Pasadena, the Egg Monsters from Mars, and Curly the Skeleton. From Stine's work—about which hovering parents felt ambivalent, given its horror and violence—they learned what might await kids on strange vacations or in new neighborhoods. Fortunately they have also grown up with caller ID, so they could see at a glance whether it might be friend or foe on the line. Stuff supposedly meant for them as kids has sometimes bled into the adult world, so Ren and Stimpy, an asthmatic dog and a dumb cat, sometimes reeked of cruelty, psychosis, and scatology. Cartoons like these seemed to need a rating for appropriateness. The grown-ups liked them at least as much as the kids.

They also loved the reassuring John Kimble, the "kindergarten cop" with Arnold Schwarzenegger's charming Old World accent, who managed to be both a winsome teacher and a skilled official enemy of drug dealers. Beethoven the Saint Bernard was as victorious in films as he was adorable, despite the vows of his overly fussy and workaholic owner to get rid of him. Raffi, the troubadour of the kindergarten set, taught them in song all about little ducks who wandered over hills and too far away— until old Mother Duck lovingly put an end to *that*. They might have left their mechanized Gigapets in the lettuce section of the grocery store and wept until their parents found them, because you had to feed them every day or they'd die. The boys have wanted to be like Mike and then, later, like Kobe, while the girls have wanted to be like some version of Barbie, and then, later, like Buffy. Peer role models have included the kids on

Nickelodeon's *Zoey 101*, costarring their contemporary, Jamie Lynn Spears (sister of singer Britney, whom they think of as from another generation), and those on *Ned's Declassified School Survival Guide*, costarring another of their contemporaries, Daniel Curtis Lee. Both series have been set in California schools, and members of the class of 2009 have grown up learning about crushes and cliques, tolerance and loyalty, from the sitcom goings on at Pacific Coast Academy and the James K. Polk Middle School.

Ms. Spears, because of her teenage pregnancy—one that previous generations would have referred to as "out of wedlock"—has hardly told a cautionary tale for the class of 2009. The younger sister of a pop idol for the class's older siblings, she has never married the father of little Maddie Briann.

They've matured with older siblings teasing them with tricks and feints and then yelling "Psych!" at them in triumph. But they have invented their own discourse, such as the pervasive "emo," which refers to the exaggerations of overly melodramatic and self-victimizing friends. They were too young to remember much, if anything, about Waco or Oklahoma City. Their first national trauma was the attacks on the World Trade Center and the Pentagon on September 11, 2001. By then, the Cuban Missile Crisis was from another century, missed even by many of their parents. But their mom and dad had not missed the Cold War in general. The class of 2009 has missed it—all of it.

That war was a preeminent reality for previous generations. The generation that came of age in the 1960s thought it dangerously absurd, and saw it as one more insane and moribund thing to be protested, along with sexual abstinence, comprehensible song lyrics, and racial bias. The next generation thought the whole question of whether it was better to be dead than red was ridiculous, and they lived through a time in which people all over the world simply "declared" their own backyards to be nuclear-free zones. The generation just ahead of the class of 2009 was starting its teenage years when the Cold War ended, but the class of 2009 has grown up asking, "What Berlin Wall— and how do you contain a population within a wall?"

What has replaced the Cold War theme that so dominated the previous three generations of Americans? If the question had been asked just a few years earlier, the answer would have been a "new world order" and "a largely successful and peaceable society." To be sure, even before the Great Recession that undermined their senior year caused members of the class of 2009 to wonder if they were doomed to be like the impoverished class of 1931, there had been rumble stripes on the national road. The dot-com bubble popped when they were nine; when they were ten, young men convinced of their destiny to mate with virgins in Paradise flew commercial planes into prominent buildings. Air travel and even shopping malls became palpably tense for a while, and their high school years were marked by what seemed to be colossal failures by the federal government following the invasion of Iraq in 2003 and Hurricane Katrina in 2005. Meanwhile, some prophets, including experts in various fields, were warning that America's public schools lacked enterprise and accountability, that the nation's prosperity was really chimerical, and that melting icebergs would someday raise coast water levels such that the carnage from 9/11 would look like a mere auto wreck.

But all of these challenges and admonitions occurred in a society that remained largely safe and prosperous, or so it has seemed. Housing prices and the Dow Jones average were always ascending. Most of the young men and women dying in the Middle East or Asia had volunteered to serve. There have been no more catastrophic terrorist events on American soil. Above all, high technology has continued to work a magic that, to them, has always seemed quite routine.

* * * *

As members of the class of 2009 grew from infants to toddlers to children, they happily inherited a world in which they considered the ability to be wireless but still connected almost a birthright. Even the previous generation had not been so joyfully baptized in digital technology. *That* generation growing up had still used pay phones and landlines. They had to wait their turn for the desktop computer at home and to print documents on the dot-matrix printer at school, and they had not yet perfected a textspeak vocabulary consisting of such argot as LOL and PAW. Not so the class of 2009, which has never thought it odd or wondrous that every medium seemed to go, like lemmings, to the computer, which was becoming smaller and smaller. They could listen to the radio, watch TV reruns, play recordings, surf the web, or read a book on devices no larger than tiny transistor radios used to be. One parent, hovering as his son used his iPhone, remarked, "You know, you can also talk to people on that thing."

They may well become the most cosmopolitan generation ever. In a society where families move often and switch religions frequently, and where "Independent" is just as important as "Democrat" or "Republican," members of the class of 2009 come not from cities or states or regions or religions or political parties but from websites. They have always thought it no big deal that there are McDonald's restaurants in Russia, China, and even Albania and Tibet. Their broad-minded perspective is the product of three relatively recent developments: the Internet, awash in information on any subject; globalization, carrying products from everywhere to everywhere; and tolerance, imposed by law and encouraged by peer pressure. As a result, they are in possession of pragmatism and flexibility. But while they are less dogmatic, they lack a set of firm principles that might guide their everyday lives. The price of exposure to an endless stream of diverse information may be a lot of confusion and a lack of prolonged focus. If this bewilderment and complexity are part of the age-old process of growing up, the class of 2009 is the first to have gone through it primarily in front of a computer screen!

The computer has always been king. One of their class members, Jay Greenberg, hailed by a Juilliard teacher as a composer prodigy on the scale of Mozart and Mendelssohn, writes nary an ingenious note without one. They have never gotten lost using a card catalogue. Few of them have ever "written" a letter, and those who have no longer know how to write in cursive. Upon seeing a set of encyclopedias, one of them wondered why on earth they would have "printed out the whole thing." They have rarely, if ever, seen a credit card read by anything other than an electronic device. Confronted with a dial telephone, they have pushed on the holes in vain and looked up quizzically. Shown a "portable" 45 rpm record player, they have marveled at its quaint technology, as though they were admiring a fossil, but then asked how anyone managed to jog with *that*. And why would you need a fax machine? It seems so redundant, so eighties. Round-screen computer monitors, as opposed to the new flat ones, have become about as high-tech as a broom compared to a robotic vacuum cleaner.

News has always been on all the time, and the idea of watching the evening network news roundup in order to get the news of the day would seem to be as medieval as walking five miles when you could take a car or the subway. In fact, on TV they get most of their news from Jon Stewart and Stephen Colbert of Comedy Central, MTV, and the late late night TV show hosts—the only "newscasters" who "get" that most politicians are lying scoundrels or at least hyping hypocrites. The satirical and zany *Onion* is more popular than the *New York Times*. Theirs is predominantly the humor of postmodern irony. "Off the hook" has never had anything to do with a telephone. What hooks? They've grown up texting "1 n other." Paper maps no longer guide the way, and they will never file a paper tax return. On a single laptop or BlackBerry they can "write" a paper, listen to music, and do an IM chat with a friend at the same time. Perhaps there will someday be, for their generation, a Guinness world record for multitasking.

They've never minded that a latté or a cappuccino has always taken longer to make than a milkshake did for their parents, because they have always been able to do something on the iPhone or cell phone or laptop while they waited. Yet relatively few have ever waited on them, for they have never known what it was like to drive into a service station and say "Fill 'er up" or "Check under the hood." They have met Customer Service, and it is *they*, for they have always shopped and ordered online. While they continue to get a lot of knowledge from listening to teachers and reading books, they have been liberated by their laptops into becoming instant autodidacts. They've always learned a hell of a lot on their own and have let their mouse, not their fingers, do the walking—make that surfing. But they themselves can surely walk and surf at once.

They are the most informed and mediated generation in the history of the world. Walking to class or back home might have once been a time to observe life and smell the flowers. No longer. Now it is a time to listen to music or books or text a friend across the street or across the world. They've never considered tattoos vulgar. They're just new ways of sending and receiving messages, whether the symbol be a semicolon or a tulip. "Cells" have apparently never had anything to do with jails or secret organizations. They prefer sophomoric Conan to avuncular Jay.

Now that they are about to enter college, they will go to schools that only a few years back boasted that they had private phones in every residence hall room. Such phones now go unused and will soon be ripped out. College deans who wish to get in touch with students by phone now are challenged and wind up sending a note.

* * * *

Privacy, for them, has always been something about which people of various ages have been very exercised—or to which they have been deeply indifferent. After the horrific events of September 11, 2001, civil libertarians worried about federal snooping into telephone calls and even library records. But only recently have members of the class of 2009 shown any concern for privacy, and that is only because networking sites such as Facebook have become concerned about who can and cannot look at subscribers' pages. Before that, parents —but not students—worried that anyone could access information about the plans and thoughts of vulnerable young people. Even so, there is a high level of trust on such sites, as young subscribers don't seem to mind sharing with "friends" their more intimate thoughts and pictures. Apparently the very convenience of, and addiction to, digital technology have outweighed any concerns about its downsides, such as widespread access to personal information that could be misused.

As American skills in reading and math have dropped measurably in comparison with those of other countries, educators hope that this class, and subsequent ones, will be more adept than their predecessors in the use of information technology to solve previously unscripted problems. At a time when Chinese and Indian students are veritable monks, devoted worshipfully to their studies, members of the class of 2009 in America spend many hours every week partaking of the diversions of the digital age. They text, they chat, they surf—they do not, relatively speaking, study. Educators are not hoping to turn them into members of an educational monastery —no chance of that in twenty-first-century America—but rather to depend upon their skills in collaboration and high-tech self-starting, primed by having spent all their lives on a computer. Hence what they achieve in creative problem solving may offset what they lack in rote-memory concentration. Perhaps what seems missing in the test scores will be amply evident in the hands-on results.

It is as though digital information has always been their friend, and the content has always been secondary to the process. Yet it has been a buddy, not a miracle. It is a miracle only for older folks. However much the Internet and iPhones may seem magical to people of a certain age, they are basic necessities to members of the class of 2009 and their ilk. A talking dog that can quote Shakespeare is amazing unless one has grown up with a lot of talking dogs. The class of 2009 has proven that even magic can seem quite ordinary, just as, by 1930 or so, "horseless carriages" seemed routine.

They have never been bothered by the sheer rapidity of cultural change. That young Britney Spears is now considered a "classic" rock singer does not bother them. They have no sense of having been left behind by constant change—not yet. That Facebook has supplanted MySpace and been passed on to their parents and to younger siblings for their applications—already—is of no great moment to them. They have already found their own communications networks and recognize that in just a few years Internet terms like "friend" (a verb!) and "tweet" will be obsolete. It doesn't faze them. Discontinuity seems normal. They await it, as they would an interesting guest certain to arrive.

* * * *

Until their senior year in high school, when the distinct possibility of a great economic collapse, with its danger of revolutionary depletions, began to intrude, they had always been part of a generation that has had definite aspirations. Members of their generation have always realized that advanced education will be necessary for them in order to compete in an increasingly specialized job market, but once in the job they have always hoped that the technology on the site would be fast and efficient and the latest. They have always expected that they would be working collaboratively. They have always expected that their jobs would involve the creative collecting and synthesizing of indefinite but large amounts of electronic information. They have always hoped for "flex hours" because, after all, they have always been able to carry school projects with them on laptops by leaving it online and accessing it wherever and whenever they wished.

Especially if they were upper middle class, they have aspired to be able to work in hip cities such as Seattle or Denver or Houston or Chicago or Tokyo, and have always wanted to avoid Cleveland or Buffalo or Milwaukee or Scranton. They have always wondered, though, if Seattle or Denver or Chicago or Tokyo—and above all, New York and San Francisco—wouldn't be too expensive, in which case they might have to compromise and take something in St. Louis or Raleigh-Durham. They have always expected to work long, if discontinuous, hours, including weekends, and to change jobs and maybe even careers many times. Having been exposed from the beginning to a culture where different ethnicities and skin colors and genders and lifestyles are routine—where words like "waitperson" and "ageism" and "chairperson" have been as routine as "whiteboard" and "erasable markers" and "movable desks"—they expect to continue living and working in just such a multicultural realm until nearly the end of their lives, something that at their age they can scarcely imagine.

They may well become the most revolutionary nonrevolutionary generation in a long while. If "revolutionary" is defined as a generation of young people who are promiscuous, bearded, miniskirted, halter-topped, and screaming in the streets, then the class of 2009 isn't revolutionary at all.

They are mostly nice kids. Unlike their forebears, they never needed to protest restrictions on their sex lives or their wish to live with someone of the opposite sex; there was little censorship of what information they consumed, and many didn't have to deal with parents who thought blacks and gays and women were trying to get ahead too fast and in the wrong way. Their parents, shaped by the sixties and seventies, have a set of values different from those of *their* parents. Blessed with the ending of the Cold War, the members of this class have never had to object collectively to the seeming madness of that atomic High Noon. Free from the military draft, they've never had to go to war unless they really wanted to. One commentator has called them "the Organization Kids," student government types who have never really had reason to want to change anything that was immediately bugging them. They have grown up in a society that was largely free of the kinds of societal tensions experienced by earlier generations.

Yet for all that nonrevolutionary lack of fervor, perhaps supported by a sort of lackadaisical irony, they may be *quietly* on their way to becoming a revolutionary generation, due in part to the very thing that marked them as seemingly tame: their willingness to organize and collaborate. They have cut their teeth on a pedagogical style that emphasized nonattached desks that could be moved into circles for subcommittee learning. Their generation has seen the end of the lecture as the most dominant style of education and has seen the normalizing of group learning and libraries transformed into information centers where silence is no longer golden. As a result, they're good at assigning tasks, listening to peers, and blending diverse outcomes. Globalization and the World Wide Web have made them cosmopolitan and ready for change. And they are utterly wired, one to another.

They neither shout angrily as the boomers did nor withdraw sullenly as the Xers did. They organize and network to a degree never seen before. They are hyperaware of the need for cleaner air, sustainable growth, healthier diets, and more equal consumption of the planet's bounty. And they may well be able to organize information—and coordinated human capital—in order to revolutionize dedicated approaches to these nagging social and economic difficulties. As they begin college, though, no one can say for sure whether they will become a heroic, ecologically conscious, school-reforming, and poverty-reducing generation—a superorganized version of Bill Gates, whose software did so much to make them what they have become—or a lost generation, overwhelmed by a more or less permanent recession and the evaporation of opportunities.

* * * *

Alas, as they left high school and were beginning to enter college or university, something big does appear to have happened. This is something that is potentially far more damaging than the collapse of the Twin Towers in 2001 and the subsequent war on terrorism. It is something that threatens to disrupt their trajectory for the rest of their lives, their progression as tolerant, innovative, collaborative kids on their way to a good high-tech job with flex hours and many years of electronic companionship, organic food, meaningful consumption, and global causes. They are now hearing about this menace big-time, and it's being called the Great Recession. As they understand it, this calamity began when large financial houses made risky bets on millions of Americans who were living beyond their means and relying on the increasing values of their homes to make ends meet. As a result, trillions of dollars have been exposed as imaginary, and "under water" refers not to deep-sea diving but rather to living in a house that's worth much less than what you paid for it.

Right away, members of the class of 2009 realize this may profoundly affect their job prospects now or four years hence. They're told that there may be high unemployment for a long, long time. Once they graduate from college and start looking for work, they may have to take Cleveland (or even Des Moines or La Crosse) after all, or stay at home with their parents, whose own job security isn't necessarily the greatest, longer than they all would like. As money gets harder to borrow, learning may be harder to come by. Might this class of 2009— college class of 2013—become shadowed by a long economic downturn rather than energized by a new high-tech heroism? Nobody knows. They have youth on their side—a formidable weapon with which to go to battle, even if that just means waiting things out or retreating before the big push forward. After all, having grown up with relentless change, they have come to expect it. And part of that change may mean that they will learn more about the dreary realities of economics than they ever expected. On occasion they hear that theirs may become a "chump" generation, paying higher taxes in order to support the retirement and welfare entitlements of the populous boomer generation whose members are about forty years older than they.

Some of the more prescient members of the class of 2009 may wonder where all this will lead. It's clear that members of the older generation, including their own parents, are quite

angry over this financial mess. While they, the kids, remain in
favor of a globally wired, cosmopolitan, and tolerant world, they
sense their elders turning more inward—anxious about their
own incomes, more resentful of immigrants, and more fretful
about America rather than the planet itself. They may wonder if
someday they won't resent an older generation that does not
share their values and yet insists that they foot the bill, via
higher taxes, to make sure their elders have enough Social Security and Medicare.

Therefore they may need all the empathy and pluck that
they can find. Will their much-vaunted flexibility, self-education,
networking, and high self-esteem see them through? Or will
their childhoods, in which their parents programmed their
afternoons and weekends with soccer practice and violin lessons
and insisted on their wearing bike helmets, and their teenage
years of eagerly mutual support on Facebook, make them ill
equipped to deal with a school of hard knocks?

* * * *

The questions linger. Will their frustrated elders become only a
distant memory as the class of 2009 returns for its twentieth
high school reunion? When will the economy put behind it the
lingering effects of the Great Recession—chronic unemployment, underfunded entitlements, and soaring federal deficits?
Will the class, in ten or fifteen years, already have succeeded in
making the oceans cooler, the air more pristine, the schools
more accountable, the dependence on fossil fuels much less
great—or will they inherit a less prosperous land that has with-
drawn from such tasks, the better to take care of the vanishing

middle class first of all? Can their country afford *not* to achieve those larger goals?

Members of the class of 2009, in bars and seminars and parks and living rooms, will soon be asking these questions in their own way, even if they can't yet answer them. The future's precise outlines are never ours to see. That will not stop us, or them, from trying to peer into the dim and misty distance.

They've Never Needed
a Key
for Anything

M ost members of the class of 2026 were born in 2008. They will graduate from college in 2030.

Their classmates might include Tripp Palin-Johnston, Sunday Rose Kidman Urban, Gia Zavala Damon, or the Jolie-Pitt twins.

George Carlin, Charlton Heston, Gerald Ford, and Tim Russert have always been dead.

Mindset List

1. Their parents claim their lives are contained on those little metallic discs in plastic cases stashed away in the attic, but there is no place to play them anymore.

2. With a large percentage of them having immigrant parents, and with cosmologists' confirmation of life elsewhere in the universe, they have always been more concerned about confronting *real* aliens than about harmless illegal ones crossing land borders.

3. Only Special Home Delivery Priority Mail is ever delivered to the house.

4. They have always tried to keep track of their parents and grandparents by searching old Facebook accounts that the folks still think are pretty cool.

5. Convenience stores have always sold rechargeable fuel batteries and offered emergency plug-in stations for vehicles.

6. They have never seen a folded paper roadmap, a paper medical record, a printed phonebook, or a check.

7. Africa has always been a major competitor of Latin America as a supplier of vegetables and fruits to the American dinner table.

8. The only network news program they have ever seen is the *NewsHour with Jon Stewart* on PBS.

9. Many in the class have been in therapy dealing with their parents' stories about how their lives fell apart the year they were born.

10. Their college textbooks are all online, rented for a semester, and downloaded to their digital readers.

11. Lucky students are driving GMWs, but most can only afford Fordondas or a generic store brand like a Sears pickup truck or a Best Buy Beetle.

12. They have never needed to put an actual key in a lock to enter a building or a car.

13. Carpal thumb syndrome is a universal malady that afflicts mostly adolescents.

14. The former flagship TV networks have been relegated to emergencies, sports, and local news.

15. When they vote in their first presidential election in 2028 they will have a week in which to vote online.

16. The Cuban economy has been booming ever since U.S. manufacturing jobs began moving to cheaper factories there.

17. Most people access the Internet via mobile handheld devices rather than from desk or laptop computers.

18. Most students entering college will never set foot on the campus from which they will graduate.

19. Thanks to their official genetic fingerprint card recorded before they entered school, their spit alone guarantees that they are who they say they are.

20. You can tell the brand of an electric car by the odd artificial sounds they are legally required to make so people can hear them coming.

21. When they bought their first car, they had to choose a corporate logo for their license plates.

22. As a result of the new MedChip implant behind the ear, any doctor or pharmacist with

a handheld computer can pull up their health
history and vital signs.

23.   Few people admit to watching it, but the hot
new TV download is the Funeral and
Wedding Channel.

24.   It is now acceptable to sing the
national anthem in either Spanish or
English.

25.   Declaring it safer than aspirin, doctors have
always prescribed marijuana for the slightest
pain.

26.   They have never changed a lightbulb.

27.   Bells playing hymns from church steeples
and muezzins' calls to prayer at the
local mosque have always been silenced
by a decision of the U.S. Supreme Court
regarding religious use of the public
airwaves.

28.   They have never needed to remember a
phone number to make a call.

29.   Federal applications required when applying
for credit cards mean that the government
can cut off credit based on income tax return
information.

30. Redheads, blondes, and brunettes have always been able to change their hair color through genetically engineered "makeover" surgery.

31. With the elimination of SAT and ACT tests, they can gain an advantage by submitting their genetic maps with their college applications.

32. They have never known a white male president of the United States.

33. With constant airline mergers, there is now just one U.S. airline, a public-private corporation called National Air and derisively referred to as "Gnat Air."

34. Lights and home appliances are generally voice-activated.

35. Bar soap has all but disappeared, as bottled soap is now okay for even the most masculine of men.

36. With the availability of detailed personal genetic information, they have always had a good idea of what their cause of death will be.

37. Lawsuits against the former BP Oil Company are nearly through the courts, and

oil companies continue in their efforts to restore the coastlines and breeding grounds along the Gulf of Mexico.

38. They have always been covered by universal health insurance, and for most of them, their primary medical caregiver has been a "medical professional" housed somewhere other than in a doctor's office.

39. Sotheby's has announced it will soon be auctioning off information.

40. After constant bickering in Congress about the nanny state, starting next year their household will get its annual carbon footprint assessment from the Domestic Environmental Protection Agency (USDEPA).

41. They have never experienced a Kodak Moment.

42. Talk of a new generation of safe nuclear power plants in the United States has driven renewed interest in really old movies like *The China Syndrome* and *Godzilla*.

43. Their parents still cannot believe that the Pittsburgh Pirates would actually move to Silicon Valley.

44. Brooke Shields, now ambassador to the United Nations, is frequently listed among the most admired older women in the United States.

45. With shortages of males in major professions, universities and federal programs have long been offering special incentives for boys to pursue careers in law and medicine.

46. With "e-wallets," linked to all the owner's liquid assets, they have rarely handled cash and have never seen a dollar bill.

47. Most Catholics live south of the equator.

48. Men have always needed as much time as women to put on their makeup.

49. Turkey and Iran, both nuclear powers, are also the two leading Muslim democracies.

50. They've never seen the Cubs win the World Series.

* * * *

When Isabella Sophia Sears was the first child born in the new year, just one minute into 2008, the stock market was still flying high and the country was looking forward to change. The elections promised opportunity, and the country was charged up, assured that the economic rumblings would be taken care of with the adjustment in a few policies. But the markets staggered along through the year, while the country added a new phrase to the financial disaster vocabulary of margin calls, S&Ls, and dot-coms. This novel and ominous term was "subprime mortgages." It was clear that greed was alive and well, but once again nobody was minding the store—or at least no one was monitoring the people who were robbing it. What started that year would get progressively worse, gaining for Isabella and members of her class the designation Recession Babies.

For a decade they experienced the aftershocks of a mammoth tremor, which toppled banks, drained personal incomes, destroyed jobs, and decimated public confidence in financial and public institutions. The price paid for preventing it from becoming inestimably worse was forked over in the year they were born, when the federal government transferred enormous funds to leviathan banks but seemed to have nothing left for the ordinary workers and small businesses that were the real victims. Wall Street hardly missed a beat and continued to argue for uncontrolled compensation and lack of supervision. The new leadership was swamped with priorities in health care and wars that folks had forgotten the original cause of. Environmental disasters on top of the financial debacle and massive governmental gridlock made the electorate furious. The cost to public faith was enormous.

Isabella's generation spent the first half of their lives as innocent victims dealing with the fallout from those early years. The message they gleaned from watching their folks struggle and from adjusting to the rapid changes of the digital age is that they had better be ready to take control of their own lives because working

*for somebody else and depending on others, especially in corpora-
tions, is too risky. They are expected to follow the route of their
somewhat older siblings: to seek autonomy via starting their own
small enterprises and striving to make them lean and mean, or to
find security via working for the government and vowing to
make it more responsive. They have become a fiercely independent
group for whom, much like their Depression-era great-
grandparents, debt is anathema. As their parents have moved
often to find livelihoods, becoming more upset with every reloca-
tion, the kids have created their own world, seeking stability and
freedom where they can find them. They are emerging as a generation of entrepreneurs and public employees. Women and
minorities have risen to the challenges, while many men, including some fathers of the class of 2026, have either swallowed up
unemployment payments along with their pride or just taken
whatever job they could get.*

*Yet amid a land of relative nonplenty, with the stories of the
Great Recession no longer the stuff of dinner conversations with
grandparents—and with their own parents often struggling to get
back to some sort of normalcy—class members have grown up with
new technologies, computerization, and genetic engineering that
have advanced dramatically each year in application, scope, and
opportunity. At least high-tech can provide some solutions to challenges. And as they leave high school, the economy may well be on the
verge of a new and prosperous bubble, and it may be colored green—
the same color as all that old paper currency that class members rarely
use any more. As the class of 2026 prepares to enter college, its members surely hope so.*

*That includes Isabella Sophia Sears, now eighteen and about to
go to college, probably for the first year or so on her computer, but
certainly looking toward a degree in something like environmental*

technology that may move her forward as she is preparing the world for its uncertain future.

* * * *

The class of 2026 was born in the midst of the worst economic crisis since the 1930s, and even today, eighteen years later, economic historians and pundits debate whether it might have been much worse. While class members were being groomed for greatness by their parents with Baby Einstein DVDs and the strains of Mozart symphonies, a Republican secretary of the treasury pleaded with Democrats—his own party having already said no—to pass the hastily drawn Troubled Assets Recovery Program—or TARP, as it came to be known (and despised)—by which great American banks could be prevented from collapse by infusions of billions in taxpayer dollars. These were institutions that had taken on dodgy assets, such as packages of poorly secured home mortgages that were "bundled" together and offered at a risk somewhat akin to that offered at a fixed craps table in Las Vegas. Even if these banks were somewhat sound, the worldwide panic might well have created such massive withdrawals that no bank, no matter how large, could fight off failure. It was like the 1930s all over again, when Wall Street shenanigans masked a false prosperity unshared by the general public, until both factions were in danger of tumbling down. But "the Street" in lower Manhattan, New York, fared much better than Elm Street in Manhattan, Kansas, and similar places.

While class members quietly dozed as babies, the term "too big to fail" became a hated mantra all over the country and took its place alongside "we had to destroy the village in order to save it" as one of those dreaded and despised American paradoxes. By the time it was all over, the American taxpayer was on the hook for propping up giant insurance and investment firms and automobile companies alike. As a result, they have inherited a world in which the remnants of the onetime "Big Three" of American car companies has devolved into a chaotic set of mergers and start-ups owned by and owning other companies, resulting in their first vehicle being a generic Sears pickup truck, Fordonda, Google Car, and GMW—new names with a faintly recognizable ring. The old brands familiar to their parents are gone, and the new brands for autos are starting to become as varied as the brands for disposable ballpoint pens.

The American public retched and revolted, giving Democrats and President Barack Obama a huge margin of victory. They blamed the Republicans and President George W. Bush and, in time, formed the backlash American Tea Party to channel the frustrations of Americans. Consisting mostly of older, white, rural, and male Americans, the Tea Party felt that everyone but them was getting an undeserved break and that powerful institutions were constantly "taking away their freedoms." Included in this group of the undeserving lucky, in the minds of the Tea Partiers, were fat-cat bankers, undocumented Hispanic immigrants, and know-it-all liberal professionals on the two American coasts. All that fury was venting itself during class members' days of teething and toddling.

Soon a highly irritated citizenry started to think that it was terribly unfair for them to make sacrifices in order to pay off their own excessive debt while the federal government didn't have to do the same. Ever since, politicians of both parties have been driven to satisfy the public's demand for more nearly balanced budgets (and assuage the fear that the government would go broke), while also being forced to explain why this or that favorite program or benefit had to be cut. As a result, they've lost many a reelection bid; over the past decade and a half, "the deficit" has created unprecedented turnover in Congress.

To a degree, some of these resentments have continued to fester now that class members are walking upright and about to enter college. Although most states still have a white majority, the white population in the most rapidly growing states has taken a minority status, and in just a quarter of a century the country will be white-minority in general, whatever may be the case in places like Nebraska and West Virginia. And by then immigrants will be accounting for nearly a quarter of new-business start-ups. Already, there is huge controversy in the center of the country about the new practice in California of having "The Star-Spangled Banner" sung by half the audience in English and half in Spanish at certain public events. "José, can you see" is no longer a joke.

The irony is that there is more fear of Arab American, Asian American, and Hispanic American influence in the rapidly diminishing number of places where there is comparatively little of it. Yet some communities have managed to address their multicultural problems, such as those who, guided by the Supreme Court, passed laws against muezzins' calls to prayer over at the local mosque even if it also meant the banning of church bells playing "I Love Thy Kingdom, Lord." This has led to middle-of-the-night illegal tolling from dissident steeples.

Besides, ever since the late physicist Stephen Hawking warned about the dangerous prospects of life elsewhere in the universe, some members of the class of 2026 are more concerned about how they will communicate with the *real* aliens when they start arriving.

* * * *

Now that the class has graduated from high school, their parents can look back to the time when they were planning for preschool with astonishment that they and the country have managed to come through it. Each family has its own stories of how they or their neighbors and relatives declared personal bankruptcy or lost their homes through foreclosure. Some had decided that it wasn't worth all the financial pain to keep trying to pay the monthly bills and just left the house, moved somewhere else along with the brand-new infant, and sent the house keys to the bank in an envelope. For many it was a time to start over. Now that these same parents have regained some measure of financial security, some of them may have responded to their children's requests for some therapy and counseling, since they, the parents, have always associated their kids' births with the start of what is now dubbed the Great Recession. A lot of the class has exhibited behavioral disorders resulting from the early frequent relocations chasing employment or growing up in families that have become dysfunctional after many long-term separations.

These same parents have had to scrape hard in order to put that vast economic downturn behind them. Both parents have always worked, generally at least one of them from home, frequently changing careers in what is now a fast-changing international economy where "learning how to learn" seems to be a necessity for survival. With home values going down and the need to move to new jobs going up, a good rental contract has replaced homeownership as a centerpiece of the American Dream.

The grandparents of the class of 2026 seldom mention retirement. They have had to adjust to working longer before drawing Social Security, submitting to "means tests" in order to determine how much they get, reading up on preventive medicine and exercise for octogenarians, and needing expanded Senior Health Insurance now that the more strictly controlled Medicare no longer pays for any and all tests or third opinions—but they will hope, with some plausibility, to make it to 100.

Families of the class of 2026 are increasingly isolated, living more and more in small suburban or exurban villages, with compact "neo-downtowns" where the folks can dine out, shop, and enjoy the park and the theater. They go out to visit friends in other villages, and their grandparents have moved back to the city in similar enclosed communities, where they do not have to have cars. Many workers never leave the house but labor at home online and via video links. Telephones have all but disappeared outside of offices. People speak over their computers and video screens, most of which are handheld and activated by speaking the name of the intended message recipient. In fact, "chat" has become a confusing word, and some lexicographers think that we need a new word in order to distinguish between face-to-face meetings and cyber visits.

It is still a nervous nation. You don't go through what the family did for the first half of their lives without struggling to regain your sense of faith in the future. Their reaction to the uncertainty of their early years has changed the way they think about saving, debt, credit, and other factors that had played such a major part in their parents' lives. But their grandparents were provoked during those years and spoke out either for more controls that would assure the country that these things couldn't happen again, or for fewer controls and the reduction of government regulations, encouraging the sense of American

independence. Both approaches seemed to generate more problems and discontent. It took years to calm an electorate consisting of people who didn't know what they wanted but knew that
it was something different from the present.

As these kids started to study government and history in
high school, the country was still split, but the extreme rhetoric
of their elementary school years had become less vitriolic. Can-
didates for public office have always focused on the issues at
hand, and now financial controls have gone about as far as people want them to go, along with a few thousand more government jobs for people who will keep an eye on the regulators.

They have grown up with an international economy as the
norm. They will soon recognize that the job choices for the class
coming out of college in four years will not be limited to a particular region or urban setting in this country—and that, more
so than ever, they will be competing for jobs with young people
from all over the world. The old advice to "go West, young man"
now includes "and don't stop until you get to Asia, and learn
Chinese along the way." In addition to the products, resources,
and services coming from India and Brazil, it is just as probable
that the foods on their dinner table came from Africa, from
which we import large quantities of fruits and vegetables, given
the decline in the availability of water in the western
United States.

* * * *

As the class has come to maturity, certain economic and technological realities have simply won out. One of these is that if
newspaper content is free on the Internet, no one will make

much money and the quality of information from professional journalists will decline. They can continue to get some, if reduced, news information on their omnipresent electronic reading machines where a virtual newspaper can be produced on screens. News finds them, however, coming from a mélange of websites, bloggers, and observers who offer their opinions and reportage from wherever. Members of the class of 2026 don't "get the news" as much as "do it themselves," assimilating a composite of what's going on from a variety of professional and amateur reports generally offering a viewpoint with a particular political slant. The few remaining major newspapers offering varied views and the last bastion of muckraking come out in hard copy only one or two times a week now.

Another economic reality is that despite questions about both reception and privacy, cell phones are too convenient and affordable not to have become an almost universal medium of communication. As they head off to college, there are several internets, some still free, that will more likely be accessed from these mobile devices than from personal or office laptops—with so much work done from home, clumsy desktop computers have all but vanished. The demand for bandwidth has become voracious, and the government, after hearing more and more complaints about reception and access, is frantically partnering with the private sector in hopes of eliminating old frequency-hogging technologies. The once-ubiquitous telephone poles strung along highways are gaining a nostalgic dimension as they slowly disappear.

Another irrefutable fact is that it's cheaper to teach students via the Internet than face-to-face. With the increased availability of online educational offerings, homeschooling gained new advocates and increased dramatically in their elementary school years. Now, it is only the truly privileged and gifted ones among them who can look forward to a lot of person-to-person professorial instruction in college. The rest, notwithstanding the beautiful halls of ivy and parklike settings of many campuses, and the Degree Management Specialists who can assemble courses for them, will have only pixelated memories of their multiple alma maters. They will complete their educations with credits largely earned on a computer keyboard from a variety of institutions, some educational and others corporate, with specialized offerings. Lectures will be on demand. Extra help will be found in chat rooms. They will be one of the first generations who have never needed to leave the house for much of anything, including a college degree.

Then there is the implacable fact of commercial advertising. They were born into a world where corporations built baseball stadiums in order to advertise their names on the parks, and bought the naming rights to every major event in life. Corporations have always been able to sponsor direct political commercials. There was a great hue and cry at the time, but when General Electric in 2016 said it was supporting the election of Steve Forbes, then nearly seventy, for Senate, and Forbes said he used only GE products and would look after their interests in the Senate because as GE goes, so goes the nation, there was a deafening ho-hum. Forbes lost, but most polls said his GE sponsorship didn't help him or hurt him. Since then, though corporations have continued to be a prominent source of support for a given political candidate, their having by law to declare their support up front seems to have limited their impact on voters.

Now that these high school graduates are heading to college, nearly half the states have corporate logos on their license plates, and again, no one much seems to care that "Home of Starbucks" now adorns the state of Washington's drivers' tags as long as it contributes to the mandatory balanced budget. The high techies of San Jose have defeated the erstwhile steelworkers of Pittsburgh, as the Pirates have made their western move to become the San Jose Chips and now play their home games at the state-of-the-art Adobe-Cisco Field, where each seat includes a video screen that allows you to program your own fantasy game in case the actual one has gotten boring. It even seems that, thanks to corporate money and the southern flight of donors, even museums and symphony orchestras now are leaving established Rust Belt homes for southern climes. Some corporate sponsorship does seem a bit shameless, it must be admitted, as churches, crematoriums, itinerant preachers, and motivational speakers sponsor the deathly popular new Funerals and Wedding Channel (FW) (tagline: "'Til Death Do Them Part").

* * * *

But such overwhelming facts—about cars, portable devices, journalism, or corporate ads—do not suggest that class members themselves have no control over their mediated lives. They long ago fled Facebook when it was clear that the oldsters were taking it over, and now go to the site mainly to catch up on what Gramps and Grandma are up to. "Doing the news themselves" implies that they *produce* as much as consume the news. They are adept at synthesizing conflicting information from diverse sources, something they've done since before they started school. Having grown up hearing economic horror stories from their parents—"and so we moved into a tiny little apartment and put your crib in the corner of the living room"—they wonder how their parents could have been so naive and long ago made a pact with themselves that D-E-B-T would be a four-letter word. Of course, while banks and lending companies want their business, government consumer protection agencies such as the National Oversight Agency (nicknamed "Fannie No") barrage them with constant warnings, if not outright cutoffs of credit, based on the income and other information reported on their tax returns.

Like the generation that immediately preceded them, they have grown up respecting difference—everyone from gays to immigrants to test-tube babies—and like them they think globally and environmentally. But unlike the high school class of 2009, for instance, they have a more respectful attitude toward economic limits and have become much more patient than their recent forebears with older Americans who still insist that we must think American—of American jobs and debt—before we think about disappearing icebergs in Antarctica. Thus for them the sort of environmental work they are most prone to support is the establishment of wind farms in Iowa and Illinois in order to bring back the economy in the Midwest, or the commercial shipment of plentiful Lake Superior water in giant railroad bags to irrigate the American desert states. Rather more conservative than those born in the early nineties and eighteen years older, this is a generation that wants environmentalism to save America before it saves the planet.

Some of them, however, have taken more radical steps, thus departing from their more traditional and nationalistic peers. They have opted out of long hours and conspicuous consumption and have retreated to a much more modest and independent lifestyle. They depend on online markets and swap meets where they can find cheaper goods and services to buy or barter. Many of them are urban farmers who grow their own food up on the greenroof. They are devoted to exercise and herbs in order to remain healthy without the need for medical treatment.

They are living in a land of the young, where two-thirds of the American population is now under sixty. And the opters-in and opters-out have something else in common: they both insist that consumption be meaningful, whether that be "green" tea (which now means tea produced in ecologically safe ways) or entertainment programs, such as the new hit cable series *Found*, a psychologically rich and intricate weekly drama about a Sun Belt family rediscovering itself during the Great Recession of their infant days.

And indeed, while the American economy has grown only in moderation since they were born, many economists think it will take off in the 2030s, thanks to a coming economic bubble in green technology. Already there is a growing market for energy-efficient home improvements, and hybrid cars now exist in sufficient numbers that even convenience stores carry rechargeable cell-phone-sized "fuel" batteries for emergencies. Despite the efforts of, and arguments about, "big government," and even in the face of rising costs imposed by both the market and taxes, there has been only limited progress in getting Americans, with their rising population numbers, to conserve more fossil-based energy. But the need for America to become less dependent on costly overseas oil, as competing nations are doing, seems now too big to go unmet, whatever the case may be about global meltdown or reduced consumption.

So the precision of various environmental improvements— from new ways to purify water and sewage to alternative clean energy to innovations in environmental repair—bodes well as a booming industry supported by government, investors, and consumers alike. The news is rich with stories about such keen green ideas as rotating wind-powered skyscrapers, thermoplastic roof umbrellas, photovoltaic textiles, "smart metering," and "anaerobic digestion." There is exciting talk about reducing global warming with machines that capture CO_2 emissions, pellets that will make the clouds more reflective, and fertilization of the ocean floor. The Green Boom seems to be at hand. In the last five years world leaders have expressed a stronger commitment to the goal of limiting worldwide use of fossil fuels for energy to no more than 50 percent of current numbers by the year 2100, when class members, if they make it that long, will be ninety-two—and they expect to make it at least that far.

* * * *

Despite these encouraging signs, however, neither dramatic reduction of energy nor advanced old age has happened yet, and to some degree the class of 2026 has itself turned more inward and has decided, in fair but not great economic times, to sample the pleasures of advanced new technology. Here the key is the almighty computer. The American culture of a century and a half ago longed to read books, magazines, and newspapers in order to imagine what the world might be like. A century ago dawned the age of the great personalities on radio, the cinema, and television. But none of that could come close to capturing the world as informed by the technology of 2026, which reflects a reality not so much represented as *enhanced*, not so much real as *virtual*.

Some of these technologies have been very expensive—not everyone can afford to get a sensory-enhancing implant before heading off to a fine restaurant or perfume shop and not everybody can afford genetic hair-color modifications. But thanks to increasingly expansive genetically engineered information about themselves, many of the class of 2026 know already what will be the probable cause of their own demise. The new Apple iPed is well within their budgets, and they can put themselves on the iPed "bike" and ride, via virtual images, through the villages of Tibet or the avenues of Paris. Thanks to computerized drawing, everything can be downloaded as a graphic novel now, and they prefer that version of *Hamlet* to the original Shakespeare one. V-Books (video books), offering audio text plus a barrage of images and sounds, are much better than the real thing. Hell, V-Books *are* the real thing.

Computerized diagnosis means that patients encounter fewer "doctors" and more and more "senior medical technicians" in pharmacies trained in interpreting readouts on the iMed, which digitizes their complete health history. They have never worried about losing a metal key, since voice-activated codes and a carefully pointed finger can handle everything from opening doors to starting cars. The same goes for lights and dishwashers. They are unable, as yet, to attach implants to their brains and download their best ideas into software format, but they are confident that such a day is coming.

Thanks to computerized genetic fingerprint cards, they can always spit if they need to establish their identity to get through security at the airport, enter their dorm, or start their car. Computerized annual carbon footprint reports will soon alert their household to ways in which they might save energy. Road signs are disappearing, since most cars come with computerized mapping, and the signs just confuse things and cause accidents anyway.

They have also grown up with a sense of disorientation that no previous generation has had to deal with. These feelings are rooted in questions of human identity. Now that computers are generating Hollywood film music all by themselves—there's now an Oscar in that category—at what point do they become more intelligent than human beings? Yes, we invented them and programmed them, but now they seem to have gone so far beyond us that Congress has established the HAL commission to ensure that computers will not be able to work with some unregulated scientist to build a race of menacing robots that, also computerized, will take over those of us who have achieved "life" in the old-fashioned, "natural" way. Will we eventually arrive at a day when computers, regardless of whether there are any living beings left, will generate their own content and have the ability to build the next generation of computers? There is always a rumor circulating about someone, somewhere, cloning a dinosaur. Cloned dogs now have a scientific name (*Canis artifactus*). So who will watch computers—and indeed who will watch out *for* them? Should they, as they develop more and more "personality," have civil rights?

At the other end of the "life" spectrum, the same question is being asked about domestic pets and other nonhuman creatures. There has long been an emerging backstory to this new drive for animal rights: the tremendous rise of pet ownership. With women now more in charge of their own economic destiny than ever before (there's a persistent shortage of males in law and medicine), and with computers being the tail that wags the dog of ever more workaholism in both genders, fewer people are marrying, and those who do are marrying later. Polls have revealed that most people under thirty prefer to stay home with their pets than go out with their significant others. The class of 2026 will need to confront the issue of animal rights, and of whether their dogs and cats have rights as persons and not just as property extensions of themselves. Will the "owners" of Fido and Kitty need legal permission in the future before their four-legged companions are put down? The very term "put down," or worse, "put to sleep," is already seen as politically incorrect.

* * * *

This generation faces a dizzying array of challenges and novelty. Yet in some ways it's an old story. People have always predicted that certain innovations would mean the end of everything, only to have other generations realize that these changes actually meant the start of something else. Genetic identification cards smack of Big Brother, but He has not slapped anyone down yet. Going to the clinic and not seeing a "doctor" would have seemed unthinkable to previous generations, but it's routine for this one. To ask whether computers are "persons" may seem revolutionary, but with every innovation they come closer and closer to "personhood." "Chevy Nissans" seem disorientating, but then so did the phasing out of Nash, Oldsmobile, and De Soto once upon a time. "Gnat Air" (National Airlines) as a government corporation seems downright un-American to some, but then so did the Federal Reserve Bank once upon a time.

Sensory-enhancing implants seem like something out of *Brave New World*, especially if you have one put in before going to an elegant French restaurant in Toledo, Ohio, but then the very existence of an elegant French restaurant in Toledo, Ohio, was once laughable. Singing half the national anthem in

Spanish? Lithuanians once had their own native-language newspapers in New York, just as Serbs did in Milwaukee. Maybe that's not so strange, after all.

Someday, perhaps, when members of the class of 2026 are old and contemplating all they have seen in their lives on the eve of the twenty-second century, their grandchildren may berate them for not having made sure, as a generation, that computerized robots could not be destroyed without their—the robots'—express consent, or for neglecting the "real" Shakespeare and taking so few courses from real live teachers. To paraphrase the late Arthur C. Clarke, if in predicting the future you fail to exaggerate, you are bound to be wrong.

We Have Always Bent—
But Have Never Been
Broken

R eaders should be forgiven if they conclude that this book has tracked a bewildering array of change. We began with an age when drivers steered cars with tillers and when the elderly might have wondered what the world was coming to when decadent young people could buy clothes ready-made off the rack. Later came a time when "typewriters" referred to women who typed, rather than to the mechanical writing devices themselves. Then there was the rise of the television set, which led to many a lovely American tree line being marred by those erector-set metal things known as TV antennas. Who could have imagined that someday the typewriter, or at least a QWERTY keyboard, would team up with something that looks like a TV screen (now called a monitor) to allow access to untold amounts of information and chats in real time with friends in Denmark or Botswana? In the previous chapter we have chosen to be audacious, rather than cautious, in our predictions of the future because we agree that overstatement is a better predictor than understatement, and that a major technological break-through is in practice no different from a miracle to uninitiated generations.

We could go on in this vein, but by now readers have just about finished the book and know that we have been on the trail of unending change and incessant discontinuity. Some things, however, have not changed and will not change.

Every generation, for example, has always been caught up in its own unconscious irony. Every generation is young once, and the young, preoccupied with making their own lives, are indifferent to the past and obsessed with their own present. Billions of old family photos say the same thing: the old had their time to be young, and when this snapshot was taken they had no idea they would ever be old. The fame and attraction of the Mindset List is found in the manifestations of this irony; for example, older readers of the list will be delighted to learn that the young are unaware that Cherry Cokes did not always come in cans or that electric push buttons have not always been available to raise car windows. The further irony is that these same older readers were once young themselves, and when they loved Cherry Cokes made behind drugstore marble counters, they could not recall when there were no marble counters at all, and they were largely incurious about that fact. Older readers thrilled to learn that the youngsters have no idea that power steering wasn't always available have only the faintest interest in the days when there were no steering wheels at all.

Generational irony does not change. We are a civilized peo-ple, and we try to counteract such irony by requiring young people to study history, which some of them do, and many of those students actually enjoy it. But millions of American youngsters have complained about having to study boring dates and battles and treaties that surely had nothing to do with them, not realizing that those dates and battles had great significance to the people who lived in that bygone era.

Another thing that does not change—that abides—is that change itself can seem insulting. Many of us know this to be true about physical change, as our bodies don't work as well as they used to and our energy levels drop. The fires in our bellies begin to bank. We lose our edge, our sense of innovation. We don't think outside the box; we *become* the box. Meanwhile, to add insult to such injury, we are surrounded by the Next New Thing and the Next and Next.

We authors of the Mindset List have learned from readers in their late twenties that our annual list makes even them feel old. The transience and turnover of cultural information and trends have doubled and then tripled and now quadrupled in speed. *LA Law* once seemed arch and hip; now it's gone. *Pulp Fiction* seemed to be a breakthrough in how to tell a cinematic story. Now it's an old movie. In saying goodbye to these once-fashionable cultural icons, we are saying goodbye to ourselves.

Some of us may live long enough to bear the full brunt of inevitable change. Perhaps we will end up like the Reverend Dr. Norman Vincent Peale, who once said it was inconceivable to think that a Catholic American president would not take direct orders from the Vatican. By the time Dr. Peale learned that he had been quite wrong and outmoded, he must have felt bad physically, too, because he had grown so old. Yet all of us, if we live long enough, bear witness to change. It may make us feel bad physically, feel irrelevant culturally, and prove us wrong intellectually, or we may choose to be open to it. At least the millions of readers of the Mindset Lists can see, through this book, that adapting to, or resisting, change is something that every older generation is likely to experience.

And then there is the matter of how American society, like all modern societies, both retreats and advances at the same time. The 1920s was a time of both prim and reactionary Calvin Coolidge and the rise of the radio, with its ability to bring Paul Whiteman and his orchestra from New York to Nebraska. The same Methodist women in Oklahoma who told Catholic governor Al Smith to stop running for president and go back to Mass in Ireland were also swooning over silent screen star Rudolph Valentino. Half a century later Ronald Reagan announced a retreat from the age of big government, but he presided over the rise of cable television and the biggest advance in the employment rights of women in history. American society often retreats and advances at once.

So while cigarettes have been first effeminate and then masculine at different times, and while "gay" once meant fun-loving and then came to mean homosexual, some things never change. Some things remain as they've always been. Yet the human race adjusts. It invents, and then in time the inventing generation becomes the adapting one. We bend. In time most of us adjust to the "new normal," whether it be a female boss or a black president or a stay-at-home dad or the use of a "mouse" as a virtual finger that has nothing to do with household rodents or Mickey.

We bend. But so far we have always managed to avoid being broken. Those who are convinced that we are doomed in the future should remember that such premonitions of catastrophe occur in every generation. Yet somehow, fifty or a hundred years later, we are still here. This, we think, is because history does not unfold in the cranky and gloomy imaginations of critics but in the animal spirits of billions. One of Ian McEwan's characters in his novel *Saturday*, an eighteen-year-old named Theo, seems wise beyond his years when he says,

> When we go on about the big things, the political situation, global warming, world poverty, it all looks really terrible, with nothing getting better, nothing to look forward to. But when I think small, closer in—you know, a girl I've just met, or this song we're going to do with Chas, or snowboarding next month, then it looks great. So this is going to be my motto—think small.

We make history as people like Theo; we make seemingly small decisions that accumulate into something grand— retrospectively labeled Major Change. And then someday the present generation will scold their grandchildren that once upon a time, when you entered a dark room, you actually had to flip a switch in order to get light. By then these oldsters (who are now so very young) will have started to feel challenged by change and may begin to grumble at the Tribe of Young Persons in which they themselves once had unassailable membership.

And so it goes—and goes and goes and goes.